TRUTH AND ICON
BEAUTY NARRATED

Lucia De Carolis

TRUTH AND ICON. BEAUTY NARRATED
Lucia De Carolis

Author	Lucia De Carolis
Preface	Ulrich van Loyen
Editorial Management/Translation	Stefania Del Monte
Editing and Proofreading	Elliott Holley
Graphic Design	Francesco Caponera
Cover Illustration	Icon of the enthroned Virgin and Child with saints and angels, and the Hand of God above, 6th century, Saint Catherine's Monastery (perhaps the earliest iconic image of the subject to survive). Author: Unknown. Photographer: K. Weitzmann. Copyrights: public doman.

ISBN 978-163901958-8

CP Cambridge Academic is an imprint of Ciao Publishing Ltd (Company registered in England & Wales Number 12646908), The Annex, 143–145 Stanwell Road, Ashford, Middlesex, TW15 3QN.

© Lucia De Carolis 2021 - All right reserved

All parts of this publication are protected by copyright. Any utilisation outside the strict limits of the copyright law, without the permission of the author, is forbidden and liable to prosecution. This applies in particular to reproductions, translations, microfilming, storage and processing in electronic retrieval systems.

This publication has been peer reviewed.

Disclaimer

The views and opinions expressed in this publication are those of the author and do not necessarily reflect the position of the publisher. The images used are found from different sources and are assumed to be in public domain. Information on the image's source and author are provided whenever possible. If you are the owner of the images and you believe that their use on this publication is in violation of any copyrights law, please contact the author at luciadecarolis@gmail.com to solve the issue.

To Maurizio, for the love lived,
reconfirmed every day.

To my father,
because he once revealed the Face of the Icon to me.

"In a world that no longer believes itself capable of affirming beauty, the arguments in favor of truth have exhausted their force of logical conclusion".¹

(H. U. Von Balthasar)

Preface

Lucia De Carolis went in search of beauty. Beauty as truth. And she wrote a book about it that I would consider essay and meditation at the same time. She defends an "ancient" approach to the conception of art, which however is not a reactionary approach – "The future has an ancient heart", Carlo Levi warns us. Above all, it is a text that defends the resolution of beauty in nominalism: beauty cannot be considered a mere mode of expression or of conceiving, devoid of any meaning that refers beyond, of any trace of a distant past. In this sense, Lucia De Carolis inscribes her search for beauty in what the writer believes to be a very noble part of modern Western thought: the Enlightenment of the Enlightenment, fruit and partner of the "Dialectic of Enlightenment".

Max Horkheimer wrote to question himself and the Frankfurt School: "Without believing in God, the term 'truth' is meaningless. Adorno is willing to say that without God, thinking makes no sense". The point is not that Horkheimer was a believer. He gave up on being. But he found that metaphysics is an insuperable necessity if we want to live in a worthy way, that is, if we want to give importance to our words. In the same notebook he thinks of iconoclasm – the prohibition of monotheisms to "make an image" for him means that he cannot say anything about the absolute. At the same time, the absolute remains the context in which we move. And therefore, it becomes essentially human: it follows that, even if it seems a contradiction, the more we talk about the absolute, the more we talk about man.

To the writer of this notion, this seems a premise of the icon. It is an art born perhaps not so much in an iconoclastic context, but at least "iconosceptic".

Scepticism derives both from God's remoteness and from the pressure of social surveillance, typical of segmentary, clientelist – and, in some way, even despotic societies, such as the Byzantine one. The multitude of mediators, conditions a strong attention to oneself, a certain thoughtfulness, the need to conquer a field in which inner freedom and contact with the absolute converge (This is to hint that it is often resistances within a society that create culture, contrary to our tendency to ascribe the culture handed down to a dominant and positive side of a given society). At the same time, the representation of this relationship – a representation inasmuch as it plays a pedagogical role – confronts us with an absolute that withdraws, pulls back, granting us only its frontal vision, that is to say its timeless side. Because time is what inevitably belongs to men, not to the Divine. So, it is as if the icon represented the "absolute" side of the ego, which goes beyond the empirical ego and also beyond the transcendental one, referring to something that precedes us, contextualizes us and forces us to take on the weight of life, of this life. It remains there, still, and awaits us with its infinite tenderness.

The personal experience of the writer of this preface with the world of icons is scarce, very scarce compared to that of Lucia De Carolis (who, in addition to writing a theory, has curated refined exhibitions on the subject). It is limited to two trips, more for personal pleasure than for research: one in Albania, where in the churches of the ancient centre of Berat there are some of the most important icons of Onufri, an Orthodox painter and priest of the seventeenth century when, after the death of Scanderbeg the Albanians passed under the Ottoman rule.

In a period in which conversion to Islam became common, the icons of Onufri recalled Christian freedom and are therefore today considered witnesses of a rebirth of Christians against Turkish oppression, in a "Renaissance" style. The distant, Byzantine divinity no longer dominates against the golden background; instead, we see the Madonna in the middle of the meadows, in the landscapes – as a testimony of Christian civilization and Christian humanism. Unsurprisingly, Onufri was chosen as a symbol against the dictatorship and the restrictions of socialist realism that dominated Albanian art during Enver Hoxha's "neo-Byzantine" period.

The other experience is that of Mount Athos, the Republic of the monks, on the eastern edge of Europe. In the churches, out of the more than twenty monasteries, many icons have survived both the attacks of the "Catalans" (Catholics) and the searches of the Ottomans, who tried to annoy, to break in, but accepted self-management until 1822, when the monks took up a position for the Greeks against the Turks.

During this period the icons are said to have assumed extraordinary powers. In the Bulgarian monastery Zografou, for example, an icon of Christ is venerated to which, a few centuries ago, the fingertip of an incredulous monk remained attached. As if the icons showed God's fidelity even when we wanted to turn away from Him.

In a secular reinterpretation, icons have become part of ourselves in the same way that we have projected ourselves out. They are objectifications of the conditions under which we can persist. And it doesn't matter who they represent, just how. Their strength lies in the fact that they keep their gaze fixed on us, observing us rather than controlling us, remaining faithful to us. As if it were their gaze that makes us believe in ourselves.

For Cristina Campo – the great mystic, essayist and poetess, who had a deep desire to visit the republic of the monks of Mount Athos – the icon, but mostly her veneration, constitutes proof of the presence of beauty: "this mystery that appears to me more and more theological", a test that man must face. To meditate on it, with reasoning, the book by Lucia De Carolis invites us.

Ulrich van Loyen

Ulrich van Loyen, born in Dresden in 1978, has two PhDs in comparative literature and social anthropology, and has carried out field research in Brazil and Italy. After having taught at some Italian (L'Aquila, Urbino) and German (Munich, Cologne) universities, he now teaches Media Theory at the University of Siegen. Among his books: Napoli sepolta. Viaggio etnografico per i riti fondativi di una città *and* The Mediterranean as a Source of Cultural Criticism (2019). *He lives between Rome and Cologne.*

Introduction

The word I am looking for is "Beautiful", connected to "True", therefore "One". [2]

It is an ancient quest, which has accompanied philosophy since its birth.

Already Plato tends to establish a relationship between truth and beauty: he finds it in justice and in desire. [3] [4]

---

1. VON BALTHASAR, H. U. *Gloria. La percezione della forma; un'estetica teologica (A Theological Aesthetics)*, vol I, Jaca Book, Milan, 2012, P. 11

2. Philip the Chancellor is the first to speak of the Transcendentals. He places three conditions that always accompany the entity: One, True and Good. They are an expression of causality in that the first being is an efficient cause with respect to objects, therefore things are true because of their exemplary likeness and are good because they are the final cause for which they were created. For St. Thomas they indicate the relationship between God (one) and all things, also preserving their uniqueness as they are held together in unity by the first cause. Properties therefore extend to everything by participation. The transcendentals tell us that there is nothing that is not good and there is nothing that cannot be understood. Original Sin does not take away the idea of good but corrupts it. Each entity is one and reality is knowable because it has within itself the image of the *epse ipsum*. The soul allows mediation with things and with being; it has an appetite that "captures" the good, and a cognitive capable of recognizing the truth. The conformity of "being" with the mental or physical power of the cognitive soul is the truth. The unity of substance, for Thomas, is the *actus essendi*, unity from every entity received from God in a free form.

3. In *The Republic*, Plato identifies in the dialectic the means to grasp the truth as just in itself and, for him, justice is beauty. In the sixth book he traces the definition of philosopher, the one who has the power to draw the eternal (PLATO, *The Republic*, Book VI, 484a – 487 aII), and in the seventh book, with the famous myth of the cave, the philosopher sees first light and its task is to convince man, who has portrayed himself as a prisoner in a cave where he can only see shadows of reality, to undertake the uphill journey to witness the beauty of truth. Knowing is a divine operation: "they will have the impression of having emigrated, still alive, to the Isle of the Blessed". (Book VII, 519c5).

Their care will be to educate to beauty, understood as a right correspondence to reality, therefore they will return to the cave to free the prisoners so that they can contemplate the Good. Even if the righteous freed will then be killed. (A reference by Plato to his Master, Socrates)

In the Middle Ages, research animates the dispute over the Universals between nominalists and realists and again those who, among the realists, define themselves as Platonic or Aristotelian. Later, it goes through modernity with Descartes and Kant, and it is taken up in various forms by Heidegger and by Husserl's Phenomenology, while in the twentieth century it is transferred to Maritain's neotomism.

It is not my intention, here, to enter the dispute.[5] What I want to understand is how Beauty, from being one of the universals – that is a way of thinking and speaking of Being and its properties, later extended

---

4. In the *Symposium* it is desire that drives the search for beauty in itself. Good drags the soul, and man, who in himself is neither beautiful nor good, finds himself capable of desiring beauty. It is in Diotima's teaching on the essence of Love that desire ignites, especially when he exposes the "perfect and supreme initiations" of the doctrine of love. (PLATO, *Symposium*, 209e6). Beauty must be pursued step by step so that it is irresistible: "[at first] in appearance and in corporeal forms [...] But then he must consider that beauty, when it transpires from souls, is so much more precious and higher than that which transpires from bodily forms. [...] after the actions, he will have to arrive at the knowledge and the sciences. And then he will see some beauty! Here, his gaze is now turning to a vast area over which beauty reigns. Oh! no longer to the beauty of one, as a humble servant he will serve; no longer loves the beauty of a certain man; the beauty of a single action [...] but by now, facing the boundless ocean of beauty [...] The moment will come when, made strong and with this light grown, you will be able to see a single mysterious and secret science: science whose object is Beauty thus conquered". (210a - 210d13)

5. The dispute, which began in the Middle Ages, saw the division of the philosophers mainly on two positions: nominalists and realists. The former proposed to reduce the superfluous as much as possible: universals do not exist in reality, only the details. Universals are things that do not exist but exist in thought; if they existed, they would be bodies, but they cannot exist as bodies because they exist in several places. Universals are therefore for nominalists a semantic question, tools for thinking without any ontological relevance. For Ockham, the universals are signs of a mental language, concepts.
There is a reality independent of our conceptual schemes, our language and our beliefs. Truth is the correspondence between thought and reality. Among the realists, first of all is Plato: the universal can exist independently of its existence in a particular. It could exist even if there was never a particular instance of it. Man's moral duty is to conform the world to the ideal principle from which it originates. For Aristotle the universal exists only to the extent that it exists in detail. They exist within the details as a form.

to entities by participation – could undergo such a decline over time: its meaning and consistency were lost in modernity, until it knocked on the doors of the present with an evanescent, floating, light hand, like the chasing clouds.⁶

Abelardo is a conceptualist: he seeks a meeting point between the two currents of thought. He starts from a nominalist position which he calls primitive individuality. Universals are logical tools to indicate a class of objects without reference to a particular. The term man does not refer to any particular, but it is not a conventional question, I am going to take something that is already in reality. Man means nothing. "Being a man" is universal. Status is the ontological condition in which individuals find themselves, it is not I who label them. Roses being in the status of being red end up in that class. To explain the usefulness of universals, three arguments are followed. The *ontological* argument explains how it is possible that two or more things have the same characteristics: the same property "instantiated" on several things. The *semantic* argument is linked to propositions: a property exists in several individuals (Socrates is wise!). The *scientific-normative* argument, according to which natural laws show the existence of universals and physical laws are necessary connections between types of things and the connections between types of things are connections between universals. (Universal salt / Universal water)

6. For the "Good" transcendental, St. Thomas speaks of desire: "good is what everything desires", it falls within the faculty of the appetitive or volitional soul but also of reason. Desire arises from entities because they recognize the good and are motivated by reason to pursue it. The ontological goodness can be essential, the one that God has towards things. If there were not this divine will, things would not exist. Therefore, the good of entities as well as their existence depend on His will, constantly recognized by God as good. Then there is an accidental goodness: the fact that I do not recognize the good in an entity does not make that entity devoid of goodness. The participation is platonic but with a difference: the demiurge shapes things while God enters directly into relationship with the things created by him in his likeness. "The highest good participates in itself, all entities participate in this goodness". Accidental beauty does not depend for Thomas on recognition, on being able to arouse admiration and esteem in others, we are essentially beautiful for God. As regards the transcendental "True", Thomas distinguishes several levels of truth: it is the level of knowledge; the Semantic one is found in the true or false judgment; and the Ontological one, the truth of entities. When in the transcendentals we speak of truth we refer to the ontological level, what makes things knowable. "*Adeguatio rei et intellectus*", the truth in terms of relationship. Furthermore, there is a *substantial ontological* truth, constitutive of entities: the entity is an entity insofar as it is thought and therefore thinkable, the truth of the entity indicates the relationship with God to which the Truth belongs, and it belongs only to God.

Immanuel Kant seems to have determined a first major setback when he subtracts any correspondence to the content, understood as a concept, from the Beautiful, as from the Sublime. Thus, the judgments, reduced to the level of sensations, end up being downgraded to mere taste and Beauty seems no longer able to emerge as truth.

Saying a "beautiful" dress still had a meaning in the recent past, in close relation to the type of fabric or manufacture, while making a speech about beauty or taste, today, is extremely difficult because the West seems to run after easy emotions, in which inevitably the idea of beauty reflects its own image as in a mirror; by reproducing itself, it gains strength, without any reference. A characteristic of the idol, where certainly a content emerges, closely linked to the presence of *Dasein* (from German: being there): "starting from its own aim [...] The idol, therefore, always culminates in self-idolatry", limited by the time and space in which it manifests itself, fixed, without any movement, and the beauty it reflects is "in time", as if it had a deadline.[7]

But there is also an *accidental ontological truth*, which is the relationship of things with the human intellect and does not depend on the human mind: it is not the latter that builds the truth. Man can only reach this type of truth (always incomplete due to its finitude). The fact of being able to judge the truth of things is not accidental, the gnoseological truth can be thought of because it is thought of by God. Things are in relationship with God, therefore the soul participates in the truth of God and operates this relationship from time to time. The transcendentals describe in Thomas a relational structure in two senses: the first (the one discussed so far) is the permanent relationship with God, while the second one relates the intellect to entities. For this second relation, he uses the transcendental *Aliquid*, something else. Each entity has its own identity which tells of the difference with the others. The entity, being one, undivided, also says that it is "other" compared to different units and indicates, as something else, the relationship. In the case of God, Aliquid makes no sense since it is transgeneric. The transcendentals are within the dynamics of action, therefore also the Act is transcendental as it is constitutive of the entity. Each entity acts to the extent of the being in which it has received existence. Hence the reflection on God's actions.

7. MARION, J.L. *Dio senza essere*, Jaca Book, Milan, 2018, p. 45

The beauty I seek is that of experience with the divine, possible through the icon because it is revealed beauty, just like the Word, and *Dasein* can only lose its consistency. It is not my concept of God, I would force it within my human limits: the icon, on the contrary, is to know that beyond that decorated piece of wood there is the invisible, the indeterminate, so full of content that it overflows my every concept, imagination, intuition, feeling, knowledge. It is not possible to force the waters of the sea into a bottle or the stars of the sky into an ampoule. Uncontainable! My experience with the divine then lies in dissolving myself in those waters and dispersing myself in the blue of the sky, looking for that Face that smiles at me. In the abandonment, I feel I am able to bridge the distance a bit; friendship with Him is renewed, love is ignited and the warmth it releases prefigures the last infinite embrace that will be. The icon was born from a need, that of touching, kissing, squeezing, caressing, to discover oneself in the desire for intangible eternal love.

We are experiencing an important anomaly: of all the civilizations known to us, the current one "is the only one that has developed in a purely material sense, the only one that is not based on any principle of a higher order", causing an intellectual regress that seems unstoppable where, by *intellectuality*, the philosopher Guénon means *spirituality*.[8]

The philosopher converts to Islam because, with the Muslims, he feels repulsion for this West devoid of ties to tradition and for how faith lives. It is weakened to the point of reducing it to a "simple social phenomenon", if not debased, in some cases (I add), to the "theology of prosperity" where "instead of following the message of Jesus, it is used arbitrarily for personal benefits and interests. The goal is not to do God's will, but for God to do my will".[9]

---

8. GUÉNON, R. *Simboli della scienza sacra*, p. 3
(See: http://www.gianfrancobertagni.it/materiali/reneguenon/biblgen.htm)

9. PASTORINO M. *Quali sono le guide spirituali di Donald Trump?*, 26 January 2017
(See: https://it.aleteia.org/2017/01/26/guide-spirituali-donald-trump-teologia-prosperita/)

Now, without proceeding for extreme consequences, it is always preferable, in the family as in politics, in the Church or in society, to fight within one's own institutions, so that they can improve in the sense of real progress. However, it seems that the West is at an important crossroads.

Economist Stefano Zamagni – appreciated all over the world for his studies in the field of social economy and, since March 2019, President of the Pontifical Academy of Social Sciences at the behest of Pope Francis –, insists on the clear distinction between the two types of socio-political crisis that history recognizes: the *entropic* crisis and the *dialectical* one. The latter arises from a conflict that contains the solution in itself: it is not necessary to question everything, we pass from one state to another as a sort of advancement, through technical adjustments.

An example of this is the crisis of 1929, known as "The Great Depression", which struck America first and then involved the West with the collapse of the stock markets. It emerged through the theory of "underemployment", developed by the English economist John Maynard Keynes who, overturning the existing economic paradigm, invited the state to go into debt. Through the help of a technician, the terrible crisis was overcome.

The nature of entropic crises is quite different: they do not find the solution in themselves, since they are crises of meaning; things no longer have the same name for everyone, and it is the socio-cultural structure in its complexity that is involved. History reminds us of some of them: the fall of the Roman Empire, the collapse of medieval Feudalism or the collapse of the Soviet Empire. To get out of it, society needs a new cultural paradigm, much more complex since it affects every social sphere.

St. Benedict was able to ferry Europe from the end of the Roman Empire towards Feudalism, radically modifying the aims and desires of the peoples. Today we are facing a serious crisis of meaning: our society needs a "ferryman", somebody who is not a Charon! What are the references?

The lack of meaning permeates every thought and every act. Even religious sentiment seems confused: in my opinion, we need to recover a vision of our own time that questions quality as a distinctive element of being in every manifestation, starting from the daily gestures, which are many and overlap each other without having a common thread, as if one proceeded by soundless blocks; unable to communicate with each other.

What is missing, here, is a search for Beauty that starts from small things, whether it is the creation of the craftsman who works the wood, writing a story, embroidering the initials of one's partner on a handkerchief, collecting apricots with their children to turn them into jam (perhaps, recalling the grandmother's recipe and the moments spent with her, engaged in the same art). The object, (the product), goes beyond itself and becomes a symbol of a way of thinking, of evaluating, of existing as connected individuals. As it happens when writing an Icon; spirituality pervades every sign traced making it an exploration, a continuous turning of the gaze, natural, without forcing. Every small and apparently insignificant sign contributes to the beauty of the whole.

The more something becomes "spiritual", the more it needs the symbol to discover its great beauty, and it is here that beauty is abandoned to meet the sublime.

We must, in short, recover the symbol in which man finds his highest expression. Man is in the symbol, he is the only creature to find a home there, but to do so we must first clarify the meaning of the signs.

We place in front of us a simple door, the one that is needed to cross the threshold of a house: we come primarily in contact with the dimensions – a door can be small and narrow until we have to bow to enter it, or so large as to be intimidating – and there is the material with which it was built: wood, iron, fabric... However, this is not enough for man. The door is a sign. It signals the existence of a property; it is one of the many signs with which we live in close contact, and man is able to move from "sign" to "symbol". Then, there are doors that open and doors that remain closed, and to enter one must knock, not only for education but simply to ask to open. This daily gesture conceals many feelings within itself: expectation, anxiety, joy, boredom, novelty, rejection, desire, perhaps disappointment; righteous feelings on the texture of hospitality, of the encounter, of the relationship. Whether that touch on the door, such as a sound or a noise, or a delicate melody occurs, we still need to listen to it, we could be distracted and not notice the touch and time could finally make every beat deaf. All starting from a simple sign: a door.

"Here, I stand at the door and knock. If anyone listens to my voice and opens the door for me, I will come to him and dine with him and he with me".[10]

The light of the world, a wonderful work by William Holman Hunt, is kept in a chapel of Keble College, in Oxford.[11] It represents Christ in the act of knocking on a door, covered with brambles because it has been sealed for some time. It has no external handle. Only those who live in that house can open. And it is the door to the soul. The face of Christ is illuminated by the dim light of the lamp. There is the light of the moon to illuminate the halo, but also that of the rising sun, the interior light and that of the fireflies that illuminate the garden of Christ.

How can we say all this, if we do not understand the particular sign that opens up to the infinite world of the symbol?

The Icon, more than any other form of art, is a sign that lives in the symbol and of the symbol. It leads to transcend the human, starting with the artist who is preparing to write it: he is not called to contribute with his creativity and, in medieval times, he did not even affix his signature (many iconographers, today, remain of the same idea and do not sign their works). It must "replicate" the different "types" that have arisen over the

---

10. *Apocalypse*, 3, 20

11. IMAGE 1, p. 131

centuries and handed down until now. Writing an icon is meditating on the Word; it is a way to participate in the divine, today as then. The face of the icon refers beyond itself to another reality, prompting reasoning to take charge of the imagination and explore divine places.

Even for Christians themselves, the "truth" of the Icon seems to be dormant, today, and there is the temptation to look within to reproduce oneself without going further, treating it like any idol. We struggle to look away from the particular to make it universal; our truth is valid for everyone and the temptation includes the idea of beauty that can be recognized in a sweater of such a brand, perhaps only for the color or "fashionable" cut, but the "form" in the Aristotelian sense has never inhabited it; it comes out in series, like so many others. There is no woman with knitting needles to make it alive.[12]

---

12. What animates it. "Substance" for Aristotle is given by a "matter" and a "form", which together form the *synolon*. Matter is in potential but only form can free it. Therefore matter is power, and the form act: what vivifies matter, gives it the cause, the meaning and the end. The act is also called *entelechy*: realization of perfection, what is in the present in act and has reached its end. *Energheia* is the result of a process: it indicates the moment in which a transformation is taking place, an explanation of its own business. In the transformation, in the becoming or in the movement of any entity, three moments can therefore be identified: a) when transformation is possible but does not occur (the paper in the printer's warehouse). It corresponds to the power, the matter; b) when transformation takes place (the processing of the page by the typographer). The moment, *Energheia*: the form at that moment; c) when transformation has taken place (the page created within the book). It corresponds to the act, *Entelechy*: the form in the present that has reached its end.
Therefore, the relationship between Act, Power, Matter and Form is in constant evolution; the entire universe is in constant evolution, like all sensitive substances. Form is superior to Matter, so Act (or cause) is superior to Power. Pure action is only the first energising cause. Aristotle thus places the distinction between what the principle of its generation has outside of itself and what it has within itself. Physics, speaking of movement, supposes something that moves, a motor that is the efficient cause of that movement. The starting point must be immobile. In *substance* there is a gradualness: in the lowest level we find the matter, the body or the material of which it is made; the *sinolus*, union between matter and form, is at an intermediate level; the top step is occupied by the form.

Thus, the Icon – deprived of any symbolic content that leads the gaze to look beyond – remains silent and is sometimes experienced as a popular superstition, precisely because it no longer "means" anything.

Word and Image seem to share the same destiny, emptied of meaning, since the signs no longer mean.

I would then like to attempt a discourse on the truth of the icon in a philosophical sense, trying to set aside as much as possible the sentimental implications that bind me to this very particular "object" of worship. My effort will be to read the icon exempting the taste – not making it a feeling of pleasure/displeasure –, to explore its truth, or beauty: it has its own language, and I will try to give it a voice through the interpretation of gestures and symbols. The "meanings" of Scripture and Icon make the reasoning proceed, and those who contemplate them find themselves having to transcend their condition in order to grasp their beauty.

My investigation will be aimed at the historical value of how the icon has been able to overcome every obstacle to reach this point, with a look at the symbols expressed in it. I will focus on its ability to draw thought

---

Physics studies moving, sensitive, and corruptible things, astronomy the moving but not corruptible (the heavens), metaphysics the immovable, the being as being; the entity that understands everything without determinations. Aristotle, with the first philosophy, wants to investigate the existence of a supersensible, incorruptible substance, the cause and foundation of everything, of a higher ontological order that is the foundation of sensitive substances. He is looking for meaning, nothing cannot swallow everything! He finds it in the energising force which moves not as an efficient cause but as a final cause. Everything is moved by desire. The energising force is the object of desire of the soul, or first heaven, which is attracted to it and moves in its direction, but also makes the cosmos move in a more efficient way, although not final (only the energising force can move in a final mode). So, everything starts from the soul, both the movement induced (by desire or thought), and the movement of which it is the cause (efficient). The energising force does not know the world, does not care about it. The act of its living is pleasure. Intelligence thinks of itself, perceiving itself as intelligible. Think about what is more perfect, then about itself. Free of movement on others (less perfect). It generates love: it is loved but does not love. Cynicism is an immanent necessity.

to go beyond itself and tend to the beauty of Truth, which cannot be exhausted by the intellect, since the icon aims at timeless wisdom.[13] It therefore makes no sense to speak of the relationship in the binomials truth-intellect, beauty-content (truth as beauty, intellect as content): in speaking of God, the intellect will always remain absolutely inadequate to the content.[14]

I will treat the icon as a viable way to reach Revelation: exploring the icon means having turned our gaze "to the boundless ocean of beauty".[15]

---

13. I am referring, here, to J.L. Marion's discourse in *Dio senza essere* (God without being), which I will deal with in the sixth chapter.

14. "Therefore, something is required, in judging nature, which makes us attentive to its conformity to purposes with respect to our intellect, that is, to try to report heterogeneous laws of nature, when possible, under higher laws, always empirical, so as to feel pleasure, if this succeeds, in this agreement, which we see as simply contingent, with respect to our cognitive faculty". Cit. KANT, I. *Critica della facoltà di giudizio*, 23. Kant, therefore, brings everything back to the cognitive faculty.

15. PLATO, *Symposium*, 210a-210d13

Chapter One

Mousiké and Myth

1.1 Poetic Intuition in the Work of Art

In a society that is more complex than in the past, "beauty" can and should have different meanings.[16]

Referring to a work of art, beauty is given by a poetic intuition: the moment, according to Maritain, in which there is communication between the inner being of things and the inner being of the human self.[17]

The creative idea brings back to the first act of creating, that of God while giving life to his creatures: free, he did not think of them as equipped with threads as if they were puppets. Thus, in this communicating the inner being – between work, artist and man, and God – there is both the free choice of creating or leaving the canvas blank, but also the will of the artist to give his creature the freedom to signify, evoke and be the object of the most diverse interpretations: "If I don't know exactly what a given sign means, well, then it is free to mean everything to me. In this sense, poetic joy and affective exaltation only become wider, more indeterminate".[18]

The creative idea should not be understood as a concept: "a sort of ideal model against which the artist's object is produced".[19]

It is a free game between the freedom of the soul and the faculties of imagination and intelligence: "Poetic intuition cannot be learned,

---

16. "So, then, you say that it is the concordance between men that decides what is true and what is false!" – "True and false is what men say; and in language men agree. And this is not a concordance of opinions, but of the form of life"; cit., WITTGENSTEIN, L. *Ricerche Filosofiche*, First part, Einaudi, Turin, 1995, p. 241

17. PICCOLO, G. *Il gioco dei frammenti, Raccontare l'enigma dell'identità*, Edizioni San Paolo, 2020, p. 24. (cit. MARITAIN, J. *L'intuizione creativa nell'arte e nella poesia*, p. 23)

18. Ibid., p. 36, (MARITAIN, op. cit., p. 288)

19. Ibid., p. 32

nor can it progress with exercise and discipline, because it depends on a certain natural freedom of soul and imaginative faculties and the natural force of intelligence. It cannot be cultivated in itself; it just asks to be heard".[20] Here lies the difference with the idol that keeps the gaze trapped in itself.

It is therefore possible to find an idea of beauty in the screen printing of *Campbell's Soup* conceived in 1962 by Warhol, but only if one makes the effort to go beyond the represented box, looking in it for the soul that the artist has captured with a poetic gesture, leaving his in exchange. Only then, only after having recognized the ingenious act of intuition that guided him in creation, do we approach the intelligibility of the work and try to understand what it meant for Warhol, what of the artist emerges in his creation, and possibly share it through an empathic act: of very poor extraction, opening the pantry and finding it full was a source of joy for the master of "Pop Art". *Campbell's Soup* represented for him the portrait of his mother and reminded him of the lunch they ate together when he was a child. Many recognized this "truth", helping to make that box, as well as the common objects that Warhol loved to portray, as a work of art.[21]

If we do not make the effort to go out of ourselves to meet the artist in his intuition, there is the risk of reducing the work to a feeling of pleasure/displeasure, and as far as one can infer (legitimize) the universality of the aesthetic judgment through the communicability of the sensation, this remains imprisoned in the judgment of taste conditioned by subjectivity, within the limits of one's own personal history, of the environment in which one lives, of the relationships that are maintained, always in some way trapped in prejudice.

---

20. Ibid., p. 33 (MARITAIN, op. cit., p. 161)

21. Catalogue of the *Andy Warhol* exhibition, Brasini Wing, Complex of the Victorian, Rome. From 3 October to 5 May 2019. IMAGE 2, p. 132

The pitfall is to make one's world the centre of everything, in the most absolute stillness.

Those jars lined up next to each other: I may not understand them, they may not "mean" anything to me because they do not belong to me and do not cause me any joyful feeling, but this would mean being imprisoned in the judgment of taste.

I would need to know the narrative for a feeling to surface in looking at them – pleasure, in this case. They could make me smile and perhaps even move, but then it passes, like the time elapsed since those years where misery was at home, mine too, and of which I still remember.

I do not bring it back to my present "in flesh and blood", because it would somehow remain in that past of deprivation: a "cry on oneself" that hinders thanks for a life that can now look at those days with tenderness. It is present when my thoughts turn to the poor people who populate the earth today, or simply the story of a friend whose husband has lost his job.

To use Stein's language, the memory is original since it is an act of presentification that takes place at the very moment in which I remember. The content of that memory is non-original: "the I of the present and the I of the past are confronted in the relationship of Subject and Object, and it is excluded that one can coincide with the other, although the awareness of identity is present".[22]

The fact that my personal judgment remains almost silent in the face of this screen printing, does not detract from the beauty of the work's creative intuition, which continues to be defined as "art".

The criteria used by other sciences to determine a judgment of true or false, right or wrong, are not applicable because in the creative intuition the artist reveals himself and it is this revelation that is to be sought.

---

22. STEIN, E. *Il problema dell'empatia*, Studium, Rome, 2018, pp. 74, 75

Creating is a poetic act for Maritain where, by poetry, he not only means the art of writing verses; he considers poetic language as a way of speaking about being, a way that belongs to every creation.

"By poetry I mean not the particular art that consists in writing verses, but something more general and at the same time more primordial: that intercommunication between the inner being of things and the entire being of the human self which is a kind of divination (as was clearly understood by the Ancients: the Latin poet was a poet and at the same time a diviner). Poetry, in this sense, is the secret life of each and all of the arts; it is another name for what Plato called *mousikē*".[23]

It is an archaic language, a divination that leads back to myth.

---

23. PICCOLO, G. *Il gioco dei frammenti*, p. 24 (MARITAIN, op. cit., p. 23)

1.2 The Work of Art in Dialogue with the Myth

Maritain knows Heidegger's thought very well and much of what he writes in reference to poetry and myth is an evolution of his thought, which he will then extend to every artistic form as a language and a different expressive mode.

For Heidegger, poetry is the place where there is no control over the word, it is the image of how a human being gives himself. The place to listen to the "pure", inspired word, which puts us in touch with the origin. It is the accepted word, which we do not grasp but perceive; we experience the absence of the word, we know it exists, but we cannot say it, it escapes us, until that word reaches us. In poetry, the language destroys the codified meaning and gives rise to thought. There is a return to the myth: the initial and final thoughts come together.

Rationalist prejudice hides the relationship between word and poetry. Man, no longer experiences the origin but uses and objectifies language, identifies thought with ratio, calculation. For Nietzsche, thought must be like the scent of a wheat field in summer. Heidegger argues that thinking is listening to where the word gives itself; thinking is giving thanks and poetry realizes it more evidently, since it does not claim to reflect reality but transcends it.

The use of metaphorical language opens up new horizons of meaning.[24] Asking is never definitive: we must consider the possibility that the foundation does not exist, and therefore never find an absolute answer.

Kotoba is the Japanese term that best lends itself to the translation of the term "language": "Ba" stands for leaves or petals; "Koto" stands for that which manifests itself in its enchantment, captivates in its appearance, unrepeatable like the blossoming of a flower.

---

24. "To be one with the whole, this is the living of the gods; this is heaven for man.", HÖLDERLIN, F. *Iperione*, Feltrinelli, 2013, p. 29. [Hölderlin was Heidegger's favorite poet]

The language suddenly blossoms, making us wonder at the extraordinary beauty of its appearance. It is a generating event that must be mainly listened to. This happens in the conversation – a privileged place for listening – and primarily lives in poetry because it is capable of bringing us back to the origin.[25] The constitution of language is poetic, it is born as poetry. Logic is a decline of language. Metaphor is the pivot of poetry, central also in ordinary language.

"Man is a god when he dreams, a beggar when he thinks".[26]

---

25. HEIDEGGER, M. Unterwegs zur Sprache, Pfullingen, Neske, 1959
26. HÖLDERLIN, F. *Iperione*, p. 30

Chapter Two

THINKING ABOVE IS THINKING THE LIMIT

2.1 The Kantian *Sensus Communis*

Not even the *"sensus communis"* (common sense), the faculty on which Kant bases the communicability of a sensation gives, in my opinion, the right importance to the feeling of the other, weakening if not excluding the possibility of learning from each. Furthermore, by excluding the content beforehand from any possible judgment on beauty, it separates it from the good: an indissoluble union in the original dispute. Judgment, becoming a matter of taste, results in the disappearance of objectivity from public life, relegating it to morality and ethics.[27]

Kant speaks of common sense in a broad sense, that is, a *logical* common sense; the common sense that is proper to the human species, and a restricted common sense, the *aesthetic* one, understood as transcendental and regulated through three maxims: thinking *for oneself*, precisely of the Enlightenment for which the man who is not yet "enlightened" is a minor, unable to use his own intellect and obliged to resort to the help of others; thinking of *putting yourself in the place of each other*: always starting from your own, you go in search of the other's point of view to promote communicability and sociability (and not to understand who the person in front of you is); thinking *coherently*, in agreement with yourself.

Content is not necessary:

> The ability of men to communicate their thoughts to each other also requires a relationship of imagination and intellect, to accompany the concepts to the intuitions and the intuitions, in turn, to the concepts, which merge into knowledge; but then the harmonization of both faculties of the soul conforms to laws under the constraint of certain concepts. Only where the imagination in its freedom awakens the intellect and this, without concept, puts the imagination in a game conforming to rules, is representation

---

27. ARENDT, H. *Il concetto di storia: nell'antichità e oggi*, in ARENDT, H. Tra passato e futuro, Garzanti, Milan, 1991, p. 59

communicated, not as a thought, but as an internal feeling of one mood conforming to purposes. Taste is therefore the faculty to judge beforehand the communicability of feelings that are linked to a given representation (without mediation of the concept). [28]

The Protocols of Zion seem to come out of this admirable fantasy, which then led one or more intellects to elaborate and mark them in good shape to make them public, directing the wrath of the crowds on the Jews as the dark force that plotted on the welfare of the Gentiles.

Common sense, understood in the forgetfulness of contents that can be traced back to values, has produced monstrosities in history: I am thinking of how Jews but also Armenians were perceived between the two wars, or how Syrians or immigrants in general are today (by most).

Art, like any type of language, has been and continues to be also a means of discrimination. I am thinking of some miniatures, from the Middle Ages up to the Canal Plus satirical spot released on the French broadcaster at the end of February 2020, as soon as the drama of Codogno (a municipality in the Lower Lodigiano area), and Vò nel Padovano started to unfold: these were the first places in Italy affected by the spread of the Covid-19 virus and the *"Pizza Corona"* aimed at discriminating against Italians as plagiarists, finally indicating a scapegoat.[29]

Getting out of the anguish of the indeterminate to arrive at the determined seems to be a human tendency, even if the latter proposes fear, a feeling useful for the purpose of identifying a danger from which to escape, as can be a fire, but the fear dictated by irrationality blocks and does not help discernment.

---

28. KANT, I. *Critica della facoltà di giudizio*, Einaudi, Turin, 2011, p. 132

29. IMAGE 3, p. 133

2.2 The Story of Peoples

A distorted narrative can move crowds and crowds are not to be trusted. The slow but inexorable movement of peoples is preferable.

> Sonia (Gandhi) has provoked a silent revolution, the impact of which will be felt for years. With her renunciation, she demonstrated that politics does not always equate to greed and that one is an Indian only by chance of birth. One becomes an Indian by loving the country, by committing oneself, and by being firm in putting the interests of the nation before one's own. With her historic gesture, Sonia Gandhi reminded Hindus that the authentic strength of the nation is based on tolerance, on the traditional openness to others, on the idea that all religions are part of a search common to all humanity, whose purpose is to find meaning in existence. For the oddities of life, it had to be a Christian to restore dignity and trust to the great majority of Hindus.[30]

In this millennium, I do not find any other personality who is a great example if not thinking of Pope Francis: he is not afraid to side with the "losers", he is ready to face the enmity of the powerful of the Earth in order to denounce the abuses against the poorest: since the beginning of his Pontificate, in full humility, he continues to build bridges in a world where everyone seems to be engaged in building walls. There is no claim in him that this is judged beautiful by everyone, but each one feels called to respond. You can decide not to listen to the call, to denigrate it, to laugh at it, but sooner or later everyone will have to deal with their past, with the "remembrance of God", and will then be free to bring Him back to the present as and when they want.[31]

> Every time you take a step forward, you inevitably upset something. You shake the air as you advance, you raise dust, alter the soil. Overwhelm things. When a whole society is advancing, the overwhelm occurs on a larger scale; and everything you upset, the consolidated interests that you would like to suppress, everything turns into an obstacle.[32]

---

30. MORO, J. *Il sari rosso*, Il Saggiatore, Milan 2010, p. 562

31. AUGUSTINE, *Il maestro e la parola*, Bompiani, Milan, 2010, p. 85

32. MORO, J. *Il sari rosso*, p. 314 [phrase attributed to Mahatma Gandhi]

The judgment of taste of Kantian memory is always pronounced as a singular judgment which, however, has a claim addressed to all men, as if it were a necessary judgment, deprived in my opinion of freedom.

Then the "influencers" were born, idols to be imitated in dressing, eating, travelling, up to the intimacy of childbirth, a unique and unrepeatable moment of union and sharing with one's partner.

Without the necessary objectivity, valuable actions will not be separated from those which, on the contrary, have no connection with beauty.

It would perhaps be desirable to undertake the journey indicated by Pope Francis. That path was traveled before us by great men and great women. They have crossed it so deeply that it is not possible to get lost. You realize when you leave it, and you can resume it before too much time passes. On that path we meet many people who, like us, are traveling and it is nice to share a stretch of the journey.

It is truly human, once the limit has been experienced, to draw a border line between what is known – the territory explored – and the indeterminate. In Bedolina, Valcamonica, there is the most beautiful example of petroglyphs discovered so far, dating back to the Upper Paleolithic, which tells of precisely this need.[33]

This does not mean fear of changes. It means, on the contrary, seeking real progress, internal and of the species: only by placing the form of humanity in its essence at the foundation of all our discernment, we can make progress possible.

---

33. IMAGE 4, p. 134

Chapter Three
Being and Nothing

3.1 Let Nothing Be

Anguish has nothing on which to direct one's concerns, it is "feeling the earth fail under one's feet, sinking into nothingness"; there is no reason for or against which to fight. It might seem a vain solution to find an "enemy", if we consider that for Heidegger the condition of man is in anguish: the "why do you live what you are living" is the why of one's own existence to which one is necessarily sent back. But the essence of *Dasein* is a "staying out", towards the future and in continuous transcendence towards material things. It is never completed, hence the anguish of having to continually choose. In discernment, Heidegger sees the negative aspect of what is necessarily lost by choosing one path instead of the other, as if the paths taken up to the moment of the new choice leave no trace. Being there, means therefore being condemned to never feel at home. It is the naked being thrown into the world, without a place that is definitely and properly its place.[34]

This experience accompanies us every day, because every day we are faced with the choice and it is the feeling of anguish that presents itself: the other feelings are always characterized by the relationship with something. In anguish we are brought to nothing, we seem to fall, we are suspended and feel the profound lack of foundation. In the feeling of anguish, one realizes that he has experienced nothing: when the distressing state is over one realizes that he has suffered, in fact, "for nothing". By objectifying it, one gets out of anguish and puts one's state in relation to something, thus becoming, for example, "fear of something".

Not knowing why, is the experience of nothing.

> The anguish reveals the Nothing [...] it is the anguish that leaves us suspended, because it makes the entity disappear in its totality [...] Metaphysics is the questioning beyond the entity, to return to understand it as such and in its totality [...]

---

34. HEIDEGGER, M. *Lettera sull'«umanismo»*, Adelphi, Milan, 1995, p. 83

The human being can behave in relation to the entity only if he keeps himself immersed in the Nothing. Going beyond the entity happens in the essence of being there. But this going beyond is metaphysics itself. This implies that metaphysics is part of the 'nature of man'. It is not a discipline of university philosophy, nor a field of arbitrary thinking. Metaphysics is the fundamental occurrence in being there. It is being there itself. And since the truth of metaphysics dwells in this abyssal depth, it is constantly threatened closely by the possibility of the most radical error. For this reason, there is no scientific rigor that equals the seriousness of metaphysics. Philosophy can never be measured with the parameter of the idea of science... As far as man exists, philosophizing happens in a certain way. What we call philosophy is nothing other than setting metaphysics into motion, through which philosophy reaches itself and its explicit tasks. Philosophy is set in motion only through a particular leap of one's existence within the fundamental possibilities of being there in its totality. For this leap, the following are decisive: first of all, making room for the entity in its totality; then letting oneself go into the Nothing, that is, freeing oneself from the idols that each one has and with which he is used to escape; finally, allowing this suspended being to hover to the end, so that it constantly returns to the fundamental question of metaphysics, to which the Nothing itself forces: Why is being in general, and not rather Nothing?[35]

Heidegger goes back to the sources; he goes back to ancestral memory, before Aristotle talks about wonder: discovering that something is installed on that nothing into which anguish has made me fall; that wonder would, otherwise, have no sense. Only thinkers and poets are able to build and guard the house of being:

> Language is the house of being. Man lives in its home. Thinkers and poets are the keepers of this mansion. [...] If we want to learn to experience its purity and, at the same time, bring to completion the aforementioned essence of thought, we must free ourselves from the technical interpretation of thought whose beginnings date back to Plato and Aristotle. In this interpretation, in fact, thought is understood as a *téchne*, as the process of reflecting at the service of doing and producing. But already here reflection is seen in reference

---

35. HEIDEGGER, M. *Che cos'è metafisica?* (ed. Franco Volpi, 1929), Adelphi, Milan, 2006, pp. 50, 61, 65, 67

to *práxis* and *poíesis*. This is why thought, if one takes it for itself, is not 'practical'. The characterization of thought as *theoría* and the determination of knowing as a 'theoretical' attitude occur already within the 'technical' interpretation of thought. It is an attempt to react to still save an autonomy of thought in relation to acting and doing. Since then, 'philosophy' has found itself in the constant need to justify its existence in the face of *sciences*.[36]

"The joy and the wonder that the world is, rather than not being" resumes from Wittgenstein. The same obstacle that a poet must overcome when he is faced with a blank sheet, a blank canvas for a painter or an empty stave in front of the composer.

---

36. HEIDEGGER, M. *Lettera sull'«umanismo»*, pp. 31, 32, 33

3.2 God Chose to "Write the Icon"

In Heidegger, the openness of being condemns the assumption of one's own finitude: it is fulfilled only in death.[37]

"We notice that science is interested in something. It deals with something. This 'nothing' you don't care about, what is it? The only thing you know is that you don't want to deal with it. In this way you are making something out of nothing, it is treated as if it were an entity" - which you do not want to deal with.[38] On the logical level we are faced with a paradox: why shouldn't we deal with it if it is an entity among others? It is therefore necessary to take another path that comes before logic; that is, it is necessary to experience the nothing that comes before "nothing as logical negation". We must meet it where it manifests itself, before it becomes an Entity.

"Why being rather nothing?" it is the question that pervades the whole of existence with anguish. Luigi Pareyson reads in it a freedom that is not related to necessity but to nothing.

In *Filosofia della Libertà (Philosophy of freedom)* he traces its genesis to derive, according to the philosopher, from Schelling's "question of despair" which, in turn, follows two Kantian ideas: the first one, is

---

37. Heidegger is interested in opening up horizons of meaning. The meaning of the verb to be cannot be reduced to grammatical analysis; the logical point of view is insufficient. The word "Being" puts us in contact, on the one hand, with the logically determined and, on the other, with the indeterminacy given by meaning. This and not this: the encounter with reality, which is never univocal, inevitably leads us to discernment. We are called to live this contradiction in encountering the things of the world, so man is on his way to being; he must go directly to being, where the very event of being takes place. Existence is not predetermined, being is built through its actions, not accepting the *status quo* of events, in stark contrast to the thesis of the given essence of Thomas. Ibid., pp. 83, 84

38. Propulsion entrusted to Heidegger at the beginning of the academic year (1927). He will add a postscript and a conclusion in the 1940s. The fact that he continues to work on it makes this text central to the philosopher's thinking.

that of the "sublime", particularly experienced in that contemplation of the starry sky which, as an imagination of infinite spaces, already filled Pascal with dismay; the second one is, instead, what Kant called the "abyss of reason", which is the vertigo in front of the infinite, the dizziness on the threshold of eternity, the dizziness on the edge of the abyss that opens when God is dramatically pictured in the act of asking a disturbing question: "Everything comes from me, but where do I come from?".[39]

Heidegger and Schelling, therefore pay particular attention to the dark aspects of existence.

Referring to the categories of modality, possibility, necessity and reality, Pareyson tries to rediscover the idea of freedom in its essence:

> The possibility is nothing but the shadow of reality detached from it and transmigrated backwards; necessity is a reality so heavy and stubborn as to cling to itself while remaining clinging to it. Reality, on the other hand, is loose and light, devoid of both an earlier presentiment and inner heaviness, neither announced by the possible nor founded by the necessary. [...] Of reality that it is pure reality we cannot say that it is because it could have been, nor that it is because it could not not have been, but only that it is because it is. It is completely gratuitous and unfounded: entirely hanging on freedom, which is not a foundation but an abyss; that is, a foundation that always denies itself as a foundation.[40]

Reality, therefore hanging on freedom, can be lived in its gratuitousness or in its groundlessness; whoever lives freedom in its gratuitousness, therefore as a gift, will be able to participate in what God has experienced in Creation; living it in its groundlessness means condemning himself to the remorse of existing and the regret of not existing at all. Reality always presents ambiguities: horror is opposed to stupor, to anguish the wonder, to being the nothingness of not being.

---

39. PAREYSON, L. *Filosofia della libertà*, Il melagolo, Genoa, 1991, pp. 10, 11

40. Ibid., pp. 11, 12

From here, Pareyson goes in search of the original link between freedom and nothingness. Faced with the problem of evil, he lists the paths that philosophy has pursued over time: the great rationalistic systems have completely denied it, empiricism has attenuated the distinction of good, reducing it to simple deprivation and lack of good (for example in St. Augustine and St. Thomas), and finally Theodicy placed it in a total and harmonious order, giving necessity to Satan as a necessary collaborator of God.

> The imposed good carries within itself its own negation, because true good is only that which is done freely, being able to do evil; while free evil has its own corrective in itself, which is freedom itself, from which free good will one day spring.[41]

Thus, Lucifer was able to rebel against God by questioning him only because God allowed him, he put himself in the position of being able to condemn the rebellion only in so far as he permitted it. The first of God's attributes, and to man by participation, is freedom: God is its unit of measure.

The biblical account of *Genesis* narrates the free act *par excellence*, gratuitous and arbitrary, concentrated in its own affirmation.

It is with the word *berešit* (in principle) that the Torah begins, as if to indicate that the investigation must begin from the Creation, not before. However, in the Holy Scriptures there is an event more original than Creation: the absolute beginning, the first act with which God, inconditionally free, originates himself. The first manifestation of freedom is expressed and signed in the Law given to Moses on Sinai, with the first commandment. *Beth*, continues Pareyson, is the second letter of the Hebrew alphabet; it indicates the house of choice, the house of the universe: the beginning of plurality. It is closed on three sides, open only in the sense of an invitation to read (Hebrew is read from right to left).

---

41. Ibid., pp. 17

> I am the Lord, your God (who brought you out of the land of Egypt, from the condition of slavery): you will have no other gods in front of me (you shall not make for yourself an idol or any image of what is in heaven above, or of what is on earth below, or of what is in the waters under the earth. You will not bow down before them and you will not serve them).[42]

I, *Anochí*, from the initial *alef*, is the first act of absolute freedom: at the basis of creation there is therefore the birth of "positive freedom", the act with which freedom "originates itself and is posed as original positivity".[43] The beginning is a pure eruption from nowhere, in relation to a negativity at the very moment in which it affirms itself, being able to deny itself, thus affirming itself victorious over negation.

> Freedom is the first beginning, pure beginning. It originates from itself: the beginning of freedom is freedom itself. [...] It is pure irruption, unpredictable and sudden like an explosion. It is this sudden character that is alluded to when one speaks, as often happens, of the "nothingness of freedom". To say that freedom begins by itself is nothing different from saying that it begins from nothing [...] Freedom is not conceivable except with a boundary of not being. But the expression "the nothingness of freedom" is significant, because it places freedom in relationship with a negativity precisely at the moment in which it affirms itself.[44]

Nothingness is dramatic like the act in which God originates himself: "it is a struggle between God's will and desire to affirm himself and exist, and the danger that nothing and evil will win".[45]

Freedom is only truly positive if it has come into contact with evil and come out victorious. This is what happens in the *Apocalypse* of John.

---

42. *Exodus*, 20, 2-5

43. PAREYSON, L. *Filosofia della libertà*, p. 23

44. Ibid., p. 20

45. Ibid., p. 23

In the philosophy of freedom, nothing is central and profound, evil is contemporary with God, an epiphany of His advent:

> Evil in God.[46] [...] Precisely to be positivity God had to know the negation and experience the negative. Precisely in order to be able to discard the negative possibility he had to keep it in mind. Precisely because he wants to be, he must overcome the negativity, evil and nothingness which are the danger of his existence. [...] It is God who instituted evil in the sense that in the act of originating he transformed the inert and empty non-initial being into that active nothingness which is evil, and it is therefore he who in a certain sense introduces it into the universe, where it was not before [even if it is born], already defeated [...], stopped on the threshold of reality without being able to enter [...] as a past that was never present and an image that was never real.[47]

Evil that man has made actual, awakening it, through Original Sin.

We are then given the choice: whether to leave the white table and be overwhelmed by the suffering caused by "pure being thrown into the world", or to write the icon by choosing beauty.

God chose to write.

---

46. Ibid., p. 25

47. Ibid., p. 26

Chapter Four
Memory, Hope

4.1 The Icon Reflects the Shape of Humanity

In the Icon, the form of humanity is jealously preserved. Memory and Hope determine the rules of those who approach it, both as users and as artists.

The artist's inspiration blends in his desire for a relationship with the absolute and his every sign is entrusted to prayer. What is most difficult, in writing an icon, is forgetting oneself, always bringing our being back to what we are: finite beings in dialogue with the infinite. Our ego must not result from our creation. The more we force it, reduce it, manage to contain it, the closer the work will be to prayer. It does not matter one's own taste or inspiration, indispensable in art in general, just as it is absolutely misleading to worry about the purely aesthetic final effect and how the work will be judged: it is a prayer, it is not possible to judge the turn to others. Writing an icon is an exercise in humility. You learn Abandonment.

"Every sign aims, beyond itself, at something and is valid for something, but not every sign is a symbol".[48]

This applies to the word in ordinary language, seen as a sign, but not in the icon where each sign traced on the empty table acquires its own need for existence, marked in that particular way and not in any other; it would, otherwise, not be able to free the symbol. Its proceeding is diametrically opposed to the daily use of words: many, too many, and not always necessary for understanding the speech, often empty, used as a means of transport for no one knows what destination and sometimes not shared.

Each sign traced in an icon overturns Heidegger's critique of metaphysics; one certainly looks at the Entity as a being, but in relation, out of one's *Animalitas*, because in dialogue with the divine; as if

---

48. RICOUER, P. Il *simbolo dà a pensare*, Morcelliana, Brescia, 2002, p. 16

those signs were dictated by God and assume the nobility of the Law; therefore, to be followed.[49]

While the artist is at work, he thinks about the meaning of his existence, absolutely inserted in the heart of his own humanity, very distant from any animal instinct. The artist who writes the Icon, as well as the man or woman who approaches it, could not, having admired its beauty and recognized it as a work of art, be able to gather in prayer before it: it is necessary to immerse oneself in that language, meditate and experience that content, so that one can kneel before it without fear of having transformed that object into an idol.

As in any other language, the problem of communicating and sharing the meaning of things arises, exacerbated in the case of the Icon by progressive secularization. The meaning passes through the saying, but it is usually "your saying".

Ludwig Wittgenstein, in *Forme di vita* (Forms of life), realizes an interesting connection with Heidegger's thought: the meaning of every proposition is inside the game and every game is inside a form of life; only if I live in your home will I understand your language.[50]

Dasein gives way to language, speaking becomes the constitutive dimension of man. There is no need to walk in language: I listen to the language I am inside.

Ordinary language brings us back to finitude, the language of the Icon is an open door to infinity.[51]

---

49. HEIDEGGER, M. *Lettera sull'«umanismo»*, p. 46

50. "It is easy to imagine a language consisting only of information and orders given in combat, or a language that consists only of questions and an expression to say *yes* and *no*. And countless others. [...] And imagining a language means imagining a form of life". Cit. WITTGENSTEIN, L. *Ricerche Filosofiche*, First part, Einaudi, Turin, 1995, p. 19

51. St. Augustine talks about it in the *de Magistro*, asserting that in order to say, I can only do it in a particular language, mine, thus bringing me back to the limit.

Chapter Five

Symbolon Versus *Diaballo*

5.1 The Meaning of the Symbol from its Origins

Originally the term *symbolon*, from the Greek, meant an object divided in half, the parts of which, placed side by side, allowed the owners to recognize each other without ever having met before. A kind of password; it designated every sign agreed to identify someone, thus allowing, in an era when communications were very difficult, to make payments to third parties, for example. "The *tesserae hospitales* of antiquity, called at the time *symbols*, that is, an object to be broken, the halves of which were used to seal the conclusion of a pact".[52]

We find mention of it in the *Old Testament*, when Tobias's father, having to recover money that was kept in deposit by a person from the country of the Medes, sends his son to recover it by means of a "sign of recognition". His father explains to him: "He gave me an autographed document and I too gave him a written document; I divided it into two parts and we each took a part; the other part I left with him with the money".[53]

This same meaning of bond, of reciprocity between two things, of pact and adhesion was absorbed by the Creed, the "symbol of faith" of the Church's official confession. It is to be attributed to the "apostolic symbol", the "baptismal symbol" and the "Nicene-Constantinopolitan symbol", among the most ancient.[54]

The symbol unites; its opposite is the *diaballo*, hence the Devil.

The tradition of the first Christians expands the meaning of the sign: Christianity has developed a culture of the symbol, out of doctrinal, philosophical and theological necessity.[55]

---

52. FLORENSKIJ, P. A. *Le porte regali*, Marsilio, Venice, 2018, p. 70

53. TOBIAS, 5, 2-3

54. BAUDRY, G.H. *Simboli cristiani delle origini. I-VII secolo*, Jaca Book, Milan, 2016, p. 18

55. Ibid., p. 18

5.2 The Divine Name

Each language is symbolic, since the "thing" is designated by the "word", without the latter being identified with it; they belong to two different natures and if I don't know this, the word will "mean" nothing to me.[56] All the more reason, if we want to talk about God and transcendent realities, the use of symbols becomes essential.

Starting from His name: "Therefore God, according to his more proper name which, in an ineffable way for us, is also called a *tetragrammaton*, that is four letters (and it is an appropriate name because it does not grant him some disposition towards the creatures, but by virtue of its very essence) must be understood as *one and all*, or rather *all in one way*".[57]

The tetragrammaton JHVH is the ninth of the ten names of God in the Jewish tradition: four consonants.[58]

---

56. "And their *sarabare* had not been damaged". I must know that the "sarabara" is a headdress: "we learn nothing from those signs that are called words". AUGUSTINE, *Il maestro e la parola*, pp. 149-151

57. CUSANO, N. *La dotta ignoranza*, Città Nuova, Rome, 2011, p. 101

58. "The ancient presence of the tetragrammaton in the Hebrew text is confirmed by Jerome who, after explaining the ten Hebrew names of God (El, Elohim, Elôah, Eliôn, Sabaôth, Asher yeheyeh, Adonai, Jah, JHVH, Shaddai), underlines the total misunderstanding of the meaning and pronunciation of the tetragrammaton, recalling how the ninth [name of God], composed of four letters, is considered ineffable. Jerome himself (or, according to some, a *Pseudo Jerome*) also observes that "among the Jews the Name of God is formed of the four letters jod, he, vau, he, which sound like the divine proper name; it can be read Jaho and is considered by the Jews to be unpronounceable "(*nomen Domini apud Hebraeos quatuor litterarum est, jod, he, vau, he: quod own Dei vocabulum sonat et legi potest Jaho, et Hebraei, id est, ineffabile opinatur*). (*Breviarium* in Psalmos, Psalm VIII)".

The vowels used to pronounce the Holy Name were unknown and Moses Maimonides (1135-1204 AD) denied the possibility of reading the tetragram "according to its letters", that is, by vocalizing the consonants. It therefore had to remain undeniable in order to be the most appropriate. "No other name is called a proper name (i.e., *shem ha-meforash*) except this Tetragrammaton, which is written but cannot be read as it is written".[59]

Gerard Gertoux hypothesizes the use, in biblical Hebrew, of some consonants as vowels, so IOD will be equivalent to I; HEH to E/A; WAW brings it back to O.[60] It therefore translates IEOA.

The fact is that in the ancient Jewish tradition to call someone by name meant to deeply know his being, to hold him in hand.[61]

---

59. MAIMONIDE, M. *La Guida Dei Perplessi*, LXI, (Ed. M. Zonta), Utet, Turin, 2003, p. 223

60. See: GERTOUX, G. God's name: readable but unpronounceable, why?; https://www.academia.edu/10728293/Gods_name_readable_but_unpronounceable_why

61. MAIMONIDE, M. *La Guida Dei Perplessi*, I, 61. Moses Maimonide's beliefs about the holy name coincide with the teachings of the Christian tradition. The catechism of the catholic church recalls that: **203** God has revealed himself to Israel, his people, letting them know his name. The name expresses the essence, the identity of the person and the meaning of his life. God has a name. It is not an anonymous force. To reveal your name is to be known to others; in some way it is to deliver yourself by making yourself accessible, able to be known more intimately and to be called personally. **204** God has revealed himself to his people progressively and under different names; but the revelation of the divine name made to Moses in the *Theophany* of the burning bush, at the thresholds of the *Exodus* and the *Alliance of Sinai*, has been shown as the fundamental revelation for the ancient and the new alliance. **205** God calls Moses from the middle of a bush burning without consumption, and says to him: "I am the God of your father, the God of Abraham, the God of Isaac, the God of Jacob" (Ex 3,6). God is the God of the fathers, the one who had called and guided the patriarchs in their peregrinations. It is the faithful and compassionate God that remembers them and his promises; he comes to release their descendants from slavery.

God's holy name, as indicating its very essence, was considered unpronounceable. The rabbis, whenever they found the tetragrammaton, tended to read Adonay; only the High Priest in the Temple of Jerusalem could pronounce His name, on the occasion of the solemn blessing on the day of Yom Kippur (the Atonement).

Even Jesus refrained from pronouncing that name. He always referred to him with the name of "Father", "Blessed", "Son of Man", "Power".

He is the God who, beyond space and time, can and wants it and who, for this design, will implement his omnipotence. Moses said to God: "behold, I arrive from the Israelites and I say to them: the God of your fathers has sent me to you. But they will tell me: what is his name? And what will I answer?". God said to Moses: "I am who I am!". Then he said: "Tell the Israelites: I-am has sent me to you [...] This is my name forever: this is the title by which I will be reminded from generation to generation" (Ex 3,13-15). **206** Revealing his mysterious name of YHWH, "I am that who is" or "I am who I am", God says who he is and the Divine Name is mysterious as God is Mystery. At one time it is a revealed Name and almost the refusal of a Name; just for this it expresses, as it could not be better, the reality of God, infinitely above all that we can understand or say: He is the "hidden God" (Is 45:15), His name is ineffable, [GDC 13,18] and it is the God who gets close to men. **207** By revealing his name, God at the same time reveals his faithfulness that is always and forever, valid for the past ("I am the God of your fathers", Ex 3,6), as for the coming ("I will be with you", Ex 3,12). God, who reveals his name as "I am", reveals himself as the God who is always there, present next to his people to save him [...]. **2142** the second commandment pre-writes to respect the name of the Lord. Like the first commandment, it arises from the virtue of religion and regulates in particular our use of the word for the holy things. **2143** Among all the words of the revelation there is one, singular, which is the revelation of the name of God, which he reveals to those who believe in Him; He is revealed to them in His personal mystery. The gift of the name belongs to the order of confidence and intimacy. "The name of the Lord is holy". For this man can not abuse it. He must keep him in memory in a silence of adoration full of love (ZC 2,17). He will not insert Him in his words, if not to bless, praise and glorify Him (PS 29,2; SAL 96.2; PS 113: 1-2). **2144** Respect for the name of God expresses what is due to His same mystery and to all the sacred reality He has evoked. The sense of the sacred is part of the virtue of religion.

St. Thomas reports that "He who is" approaches the most appropriate name for three reasons: because of its meaning, not expressing a definite form; by its universality, as it includes everything in itself and, quoting Damascene, "He who is [...] possesses being itself as a kind of ocean of infinite substance and without shores".[62]

It is also so for the modality, as it indicates being in the present. God comes before time and therefore he does not know past and future. Finally, he adds: "Then even more proper name is the Tetragrammaton [Jahvé], which is destined to signify the divine nature as incommunicable and singular".[63]

Hence, the difficulty in representation and the obsessive fear of idolatrous deviations inherited from the Jewish tradition (*Exodus* 20.4; *Deuteronomy* 4.15-18), with the disputes that led to the iconoclasm of the Eighth and Ninth centuries.

---

62. THOMAS AQUINAS, *Summa Theologiae* I, q. 13, a. 11

63. Ibidem

5.3 In Metaphorical Symbolism We Recognise "He Who Is"

Iahvé is an archaic form of the verb to be: He who is, He who makes exist, the Existent, the Being: "I am who I am".[64]

Thus, the Father presents himself, and we with him cannot but evoke him by means of extrinsic attribution analogies.[65]

God cannot be prescribed within categories known to us. We therefore use the metaphor to bring out some of its attributes: "we put a term that usually belongs to another subject or to another semantic sphere and we force it to say something about our subject to which it would not be immediately attributed".[66]

---

64. *Exhodus*, 3, p. 14

65. The analogy of extrinsic attribution, or metaphor, is applied when we want to attribute terms (or attributes) to a subject that does not belong to its own semantic domain (Luke is a rock). "A name can be communicated in two ways: in the proper sense, or by juxtaposition or similarity. A communicable name in the proper sense is the one that is attributed to several things according to the full extent of its meaning; communicable by an approach is that which is attributed to other beings for some of the various elements included in its meaning. For example, the term *lion* in the proper sense is said of all those animals in which the nature expressed by this name is found: by similarity, or analogy, it is attributed to all the individuals who participate in something leonine, such as the audacity or fortitude, for which they metaphorically call themselves lions". (S.TH., I, q. 13, a. 9).

In the case of the metaphor, we are talking about the analogy of proportionality. There are four terms: A (morning) is to B (evening) as C (youth) is to D (we could also omit the term "old age"; the reasoning here would lead us, anyway). The metaphor hides at least one element setting in motion the search for meaning: it is therefore the most suitable for talking about God and his properties. Instead, we use the intrinsic attribution analogy when attributes, while not essential to the nature of the subject, specify it (Luke is splendid); distinguishing the different species within a different genus, helps classification: in the "animal" genus are included several "species"; rationality makes the difference between a dog and a man. Being has multiple meanings and here Heidegger stops continuing his search indefinitely. The first of the meanings (and the starting point for Parmenide, too) is the essence that indicates substance.

It must therefore be concluded that these terms are affirmed of God and of creatures according to analogy, that is, proportion. And this happens in two ways: either because several terms apply to a single term [original and inderivated] – as healthy is said of medicine and urine, since both say a certain order and a relation to the health of the animal, this as an index, that as a cause – or because one term has [correspondence or] proportion with another, as healthy is said of medicine and of the animal, in that medicine is the cause of health which is in the animal. And in this way some names are said of

---

The case of the intrinsic attribution analogy is an analogy of proportion and has three terms, two of which (apple and race) refer to a third (healthy). The reference is always to the *analogous princes* (healthy). Aristotle calls it the *Pros Hen* analogy, towards one: it is the main meaning to which the others refer. Analogy of proportion and analogy of proportionality are concepts derived from Aristotle. The IV Lateran Council establishes that between creature and Creator there is an analogy of proportionality because the differences are greater than the similarities. Even St. Thomas excludes the proportion as "*relaxio non execua*" and arrives at the transcendental analogy to describe the similarity between finite and infinite, where the similarity makes discernment possible while underlining the radical difference between finite and infinite: they are not proportionate but *proportionable*; God is good, man has goodness. What happens in infinity is similar to what happens in finite reality. In the case of the divine names, Thomas makes it explicit when speaking of "good": "the origin of the term refers to man but the Good is God in His perfection, then to man". (S.TH., I, Q. 13, A. 11).

In *Cratylus*, Plato was the first to question the rectitude of words, making them instruments used by man to refer to reality, leaving the relationship between word and reality unsolved; only a linguistic question remains. The true and the false is an extra-linguistic question. Aristotle argues that there must be correspondence between reality and truth and the truth cannot be found in the word taken individually; it is necessary to move to the utterance when one preaches something about a subject by giving a judgment. Words are things spoken without connection; propositions (or utterances) are things said with connection, connectives. The true and the false are expressed only in propositions. There is no contradiction in reality, just as the discourse that is made on reality cannot have contradictions. The principle of non-contradiction is the foundation of all his theory, since you try to deny it you bring it out. The other universal principle is that of the excluded third (between discourses that contradict each other there is no third possibility). PICCOLO, G. *Fatti di Parole*, pp. 24, 25, 26, 105, 106, 107

66. Ibid., p. 106

God and creatures analogically, and not in a purely equivocal sense, or even univocal. In fact, we cannot speak of God if not starting from creatures, as we have shown above. And so whatever term is said of God and of creatures, it is said for the relationship that creatures have with God, as a principle or cause, in which all the perfections of things pre-exist in an excellent way.[67]

To say: "God is a rock", means to relate the two terms through "solidity"; the third term we reach pushed by the metaphor, thus increasing the possibilities of talking about it. The term "solidity" emerges as a "symbolon", a sign of recognition, a bond. The metaphor pushes reasoning to search, kidnaps it to dullness because it strikes it in amazement and elevates it to the imagination: a new image is produced in our mind, which enriches and enlivens those already present.

In study seven of *La metafora viva (The metaphor alive)* Paul Ricoeur explores the different way in which metaphor allows us to refer to things, which is not the same as that used for descriptive propositions, since it does not crystallize on the primary meanings of the terms, as it happens for science. The metaphor uses the language proper to poetry: the terms used here must "create a crisis"; metaphor must escape the primary meaning to suggest that the profound reality of being is not all that appears. On the contrary, what appears is nothing but the "tip of the iceberg", it enlivens us to immerse ourselves more and more in the depths of the vast ocean, or climb the mountains and challenge its dangers, to pursue and hope to one day reach the "True" and the "Beautiful".[68] [69]

---

67. THOMAS AQUINAS, I, q.13, a. 5. The solution: "God [as cause] is the measure [of entities], but a measure exceeding any of their proportions. Therefore, it is not necessary that God and creatures be contained under the same genus. The arguments in contrast prove that the aforesaid names are not said of God and creatures univocally; but they do not prove that they are spoken equivocally", Ibid., THOMAS AQUINAS, I, q.13, a. 5, ad. 3

68. IMAGE 5, p. 136

69. IMAGE 6, p. 138

The suspension of the real reference is the condition for accessing the reference in a virtual way. "It is in the same analysis", continues Ricoeur, "that a referential conception of poetic language must take root which takes into account the suppression of ordinary language and is based instead on the concept of doubled reference".[70]

---

[70]. PICCOLO, G. *Fatti di Parole*, pp. 109, 110

Chapter Six
AIM AND APPEAR

6.1 Idol and Icon

Art is a magnifying glass placed on a specific geographical area, where there are expressed beliefs, political, social and moral trends referring to that specific culture at that precise historical moment. Each form of art is an intricate mosaic of symbols that is the key to entering those different worlds.

"Man – writes Ernst Cassirer – does not live in a purely physical universe, but in a symbolic universe".[71] The sign is part of physical reality with an operational character, also accessible to the animal while the symbol has a functional value with a designative and representative character, typical of man.

The mystery of the Incarnation offers Christianity the opportunity to reach its maximum expression with art in terms of dissemination and educational effectiveness, through universally and immediately recognized symbols.

> The genius of the Christian religion is that, although its mysteries transcend our understanding, it has found a way, especially thanks to art, to translate them into universally understandable terms, in situations common to all [...]. The primordial image of Western art is that of a mother with a child.[72]

The Incarnation finds its greatest ally in art, due to its innate aptitude for vivifying meanings through a body recognizable by the human mind, and will be faced by artists at every stage, from the Annunciation to Death and Resurrection.

However, it is necessary to scrupulously define which are the characteristics of the idol and which are those that define the icon, whose boundaries sometimes seem confused to this day. Jean-Luc Marion offers us a clear distinction.

---

71. CASSIRER, E. *Saggio sull'uomo. Introduzione ad una filosofia della cultura umana*, Armando, Rome, 2009, p. 80

72. DANTO, A.C. *Che cos'è l'arte*, Johan & Levi, 2017, p. 68

6.2 The Idol According to Marion

Idol and icon are able to arouse veneration since they both admit the "*signa* of the divine": they sign, indicate a third term, just as the work of art generally acquires a symbolic value in referring to something else. We must therefore ask ourselves about the *signa*, about their different way of making a sign. The idol seems indissolubly linked to visibility, it could never be defined as illusory because it is seen clearly, it is known because it is seen: "*eidon* is what is known by the very fact that it has been seen (*oida*)".[73]

It seems to be inseparable with visibility, so much so that it is placed in places where it is impossible not to see it; it is understood in the gaze, the manufactured thing is exhausted in the watchable. The gaze precedes the idol and stops it on itself: "In this arrest, the gaze ceases to surpass itself and to pass through, therefore it ceases to pass through visible things, to stop at the splendor of one of them [...] it no longer finds any transparency"; it attracts it to itself, captures it and fills it.[74] Before then, the gaze was insatiable; the idol stops it on itself, sends it back to itself, in a place, imposing a first limit on it. The idol thus plays the role of a mirror referring to its image, dazzling the gaze, filling it: "the splendor of the watchable finally visible", makes the mirror invisible.

> The visible begins where the aim ends. The invisible mirror conceals itself in the first visible [idol], which thus marks the unadmirable. The idol does not admit any invisible, first of all because, in the splendor of its own light, it conceals its function as an invisible mirror, and secondly because beyond the idol it opens – or rather closes – even more than the invisible, the unadmirable. [...] It commensurates with what the reach of certain human gazes can bear. [...] The idol is commensurate with the templum that from time to time the gaze of man delimits in the sky, commensurating it to himself: "this

---

73. MARION, J.L. *Dio senza essere*, p. 23

74. Ibid., p. 25

God, whose temple is all you see". This God, whose space of manifestation is commensurate with what a gaze can bear: that is, precisely, an idol.[75]

The viewer's attitude must become religious in order to find in that painted table or carved stone the splendor that allows the gaze to stop on it: "The idol acts as a material link taken between different splendors produced by the same first visible one; it becomes the concrete history of the God and the memory that mankind retain or not".[76]

The concept brings to light the feeling of the spirit, but from the very moment that philosophy tries to conceptualize God, enclosing him in thinkable categories, the concept moves exactly like an idol.

---

75. Ibid., p. 28
76. Ibid., p. 29

6.3 The Icon

The icon causes the vision, it is not seen but appears! The invisible takes on the appearance of someone, without the divine being entangled in the material that manifests it. Jesus himself, his historical figure, if he did not refer to the Father, would remain one of the mortals, entangled in his human affairs. Only by thinking of the Virgin Mary as the Mother of God can she be freed of mortal remains to elevate her to the celestial sphere. Her Assumption into heaven, like the Transfiguration of Christ and His Resurrection, makes the hearts of believers vibrate and their personified images become the icon of the invisible God.

The task of the icon is the continuous reference to something other than itself, "without this other being ever able to reproduce itself", until the gaze, proceeding through the visible, reaches the invisible, surpassing itself, overcoming all its tendency to grasp and capture infinity.[77] It does not find rest in the image, because it would be to rest in the earth, to bury one's gaze; the icon does not show him the place to rest, it pushes him to search beyond, beyond what the sense of sight offers him as graspable. "The icon becomes visible only by arousing an infinite gaze".[78]

The hypostasis (its form, what is seen) venerated, and not worshipped (adoration is reserved for God), in the icon excludes any substantial presence, the opposite of what happens in the Eucharist where the body of Christ vivifies it. That painted face refers to the hypostasis of the one to whom that face belongs, in the features determined by centuries of comparison, where theologians directed the hands of the artists who in the first centuries of Christianity were preparing to write icons, defining forms and symbols that arrived up to the present day. The gaze of the invisible looks at the man, the invisible intention looks at him in the face: "The icon opens on a face, in which the sight of man does not look

---

77. Ibid., p. 34
78. Ibid., p. 34

at anything in the face, but goes back to infinite from the visible to the invisible through the grace of the visible itself; it does not censor the non-admirable, the icon opens in a face that looks at our gazes to call them to its depth [...] only the icon shows us a face (or, in other words, every face is given as an icon) [...] nothing imprisons a face in a mask more than a radiant smile does".[79]

The invisible of the icon coincides with the intention of the face that looks at us in the face with its gaze, becoming more and more visible. In short, the icon does not let itself be touched by a glance; it brings us into Relation, infinity calls us, until the painted table that we caress turning to it becomes transparent. It comes to us from another world, infinitely refers to the origin, is crossed by never ending depth, or elevation. Our gaze joins and merges with the gaze that iconically looks at us in the face: "the invisible looks-in-the-face (as invisible) only by passing to the visible (as a face), while the visible gives something to see (as visible) only by passing to the invisible (as intention)".[80] Visible and invisible, united indissolubly.

According to traditional Orthodox doctrine: "the icon is the image and even the presence of the invisible".[81] For such a conception of the image, the need was immediately felt to distinguish the forms of worship; a distinction that is found in the writings of John Damascene.

As we said, adoration is reserved only for God. "Relative veneration" is reserved for icons, as well as for the Virgin and the Saints, since the image acts as an intermediary for the one who is represented, therefore relative to a reality; it is always an image of someone.[82]

---

79. Ibid., p. 35

80. Ibid., p. 39

81. SENDLER, E. *L'icona immagine dell'invisibile. Elementi di teologia, estetica e tecnica*, Edizioni San Paolo, Milan, 1985, 41

82. Ibid., p. 43

If worship is made in the image of Christ, this veneration becomes adoration because it is the incarnate Word who is represented, his prototype. But can the prototype be present? Theodore, avoiding being accused of platonic tendencies, states: "The prototype is not in the image according to the essence, otherwise the image would also be called the prototype and, conversely, the prototype image: which is not convenient because each nature (that of the model and that of the icon) has its own definition. The prototype is therefore in the image according to the similarity of the hypostasis", stating that Christ and the icon have the same hypostasis.[83]

John Damascene argued, instead, that the icon is as if it were filled with energy and grace, transforming it into an entative participation in the body of Christ, making it dangerously close to the sacraments. St. Theodore would not hesitate to burn a deteriorated table, not so the Damascene.

To describe this mode of presence, Theodore uses the image of the seal and its imprint:

> Take for example a ring on which the image of the emperor is engraved: whether it is imprinted in wax, pitch or clay, the seal will remain immutably the same in each material which, on the contrary, stands out well from the others. The seal would not remain the same in the different subjects if it participated in some way in the subjects themselves. In fact, it is separate from these and remains in the ring. Similarly, the likeness of Christ, even if imprinted in any matter, is not in communion with the material in which it expresses, but remains in the hypostasis of Christ, to which it belongs.[84]

He did not despise matter, as Plato asserted in *Cratylus*; on the contrary, it pointed out the way the hypostasis is present in the icon.[85]

---

83. Ibid., p. 45

84. Ibid., p. 47

85. "In fact, some people claim that the body (*sóma*) is the tomb (*séma*) of the soul, because the soul is buried there, for the time being". Cit. PLATO, *Cratylus,* 400c

Chapter Seven

THE DOGMA OF INCARNATION IN THE ICON

7.1 The Germs of Iconoclasm

By studying and deepening the thought of the Fathers of the Church, one gets the impression that they moved with the same attention used in moving in a field full of pitfalls of all kinds: "It is still a question of images", a man of our time would say, forgetting the value aspect of the icon.

Instead, it turns out that the question of images is fundamental, because it is closely connected with the very essence of Christianity: Incarnation.

> It is Incarnation that is called into question by iconoclasm, and it is Incarnation that is defended in the cult of icons. The icon is the reflection of the prototype and each icon is the reflection of the divine and human natures united without mixing in the person of Christ. This principle of the union of the divine and the human dominates all areas of the Church's life: its doctrine, its sacraments, its relations with the world, its liturgy and its art.[86]

The events that marked the approximately one hundred and twenty years of the iconoclastic period are often dismissed as not belonging to the Christian West, while the sacrifice of those men, mostly monks, also protected and safeguarded our Christian-Catholic faith, and not only because the two churches, at the time, were still united.[87][88]

---

86. SENDLER, E. *L'icona immagine dell'invisibile*, p. 38

87. We can indicate as the starting date 721, when the caliph Yezid II gave the order to destroy all the images in the sanctuaries and houses of the occupied territories, and as the end date 843, under the empire of Theodora.

88. *The Great Schism*, defined in the East as the *Latin Schism* and in the West as the *Eastern Schism*, was the event which – by breaking the unity of what was the State Church of the Roman Empire based on the Pentarchy – divided Christianity Chalcedonian between the Roman Catholic Church, which had developed the idea of the primacy, including jurisdictional, of the Bishop of Rome (as he was considered the successor of the Apostle Peter), and the Orthodox Church (which, instead, believed it represented continuity of

The first years of the nascent Church were the years of the dogmatic definition of the creed, several councils alternated, first attended by the emperors and only later, with the secularization, by the Popes.

---

the undivided church of the first millennium). Although 1054 is normally indicated as the year of the schism, that is when Pope Leo IX, through his legates, excommunicated the patriarch Michael I Cerularius and the latter, in turn, responded with his own anathema; the Schism was, actually, the result of a long period of progressive distancing between the two Churches. The disputes underlying the schism were essentially two. The first concerned papal authority: the Pope (i.e. the Bishop of Rome), considering himself invested with the Petrine primacy over the whole Church by mandate of Christ, and therefore with a jurisdictional power, began to claim his authority over the four Eastern patriarchates too. (Constantinople, Alexandria, Antioch and Jerusalem, which, with Rome, formed the so-called pentarchy), willing to grant the Patriarch of the West only an honorary primacy and to let his effective authority extend only to the Christians of the West. The other dispute, of a Trinitarian and apparently less "political" context, concerned the addition of the Filioque in the Nicene Creed, which took place in the Latin context. There were also other, less significant causes, including variations of some liturgical rites, and conflicting claims of jurisdiction. See: https://it.wikipedia.org/wiki/Portale:Ortodossia/Grande_Scisma

7.2 Christian Art: Dogmas Translated into Art

The first Christians used art to transmit their teachings.

The main reason was the rampant illiteracy that included every social class but not only: in art the Christian religion found a great ally because it was able to make the mystery of the Incarnation immediate and universal as no story or code could; it belongs to the art to embody feelings and mental states expressed in a narrative.

The Fathers of the Church had the task of drawing up the guidelines for the present and future catechesis of the nascent Church.

Those were the times in which the Church had to put order to the various religious currents that appeared as a truth of faith, influencing primitive Christianity not yet consolidated and institutionalized, and which were then declared heterodox and condemned as heretical by the Church. Many of these heresies were Christological in the sense that they concerned precisely the definition of the nature and person of Jesus Christ.

As long as the disputes between Christians were kept quiet within the ecclesiastical seats, they did not become a matter of state. When Constantine gave authority to Christianity, the disputes moved to the squares and became increasingly bitter. The emperor, worried that this could aggravate the state of disintegration in which the state had been for years, decided to convene the first ecumenical council of the Christian world, according to the practice of the Council of Jerusalem of the apostolic age: *The First Council of Nicaea*, on 20 May 325. Presided over by the emperor himself, it tackled first of all the task of establishing the nature of Christ in relation to the Father: if the son were the substance of the father, expressed in the Creed, or "Nicene Symbol", which since this Council remains (in meaning) almost identical to the one we recite today on Sunday in church. He therefore established the consubstantiality of the Father with the Son, "begotten not made, one in being with the Father"; and that His coming is after the Father, born from the Father before all ages: "God from God,

Light from Light, true God from true God", thus declaring Arianism heterodox. In contrast to the Gnostic doctrines, Incarnation, Death and Resurrection are reaffirmed: "For us men and for our salvation He came down from heaven"; "He was crucified under Pontius Pilate. He suffered, died and was buried"; "On the third day He rose again, in fulfillment of the Scriptures. He ascended into heaven and is seated at the right hand of the Father".

The Christological doctrine elaborated by Arius, according to which Jesus did not have the same divine nature as the Father, was therefore condemned as heresy. The virgin birth of Jesus was reaffirmed, "by the power of the Holy Spirit he became incarnate from the Virgin Mary" – it was only reaffirmed since it is already present in the Gospel according to Matthew – and established a date for the most important feast of Christianity: the Easter of Resurrection has since been celebrated on the first Sunday after the full moon following the spring equinox.[89]

Defining the dogmas of faith was also regulating the laws of the state, therefore the daily life of every citizen who lived in that "form of life", since at that time the powers of state and church were not divided.

Most of the writings of St. Augustine, the last of the Fathers in chronological order, have come down to us, transmitting the enormous work of the Saint in fighting the many heresies that became truths of faith and the Church of today, in its laws and in its dogmas, owes much to His thought. This, despite being a living organism and, as such, in continuous growth in the search for truth as beauty, to be interpreted and extrapolated from Sacred Scripture, which is Word but also the narration of a journey: life.

Between 396 and 405 Augustine was engaged against Manichaeism, a religion dating back to the third century, founded in ancient Persia

---

89. IMAGE 7, p. 139

by Mani, which conceived all reality as a perennial struggle between two opposing principles: good and evil, spirit and matter, light and darkness, God and his antagonist. The council that placed this religion outside the orthodoxy of the Church was that of Ephesus, the third ecumenical council, convened by Emperor Theodosius II and held in 431. It confirmed the Nicene Creed.

Every step of the Church in the direction of defining its own dogmas was accompanied and supported by art. It was the most immediate way to transfer the disputes translated into dogmas by the various councils to the faithful, mostly said to be illiterate, who found the Law confirmed in the images, and therefore the moral norms to follow.

Among the most ancient representations that have come down to us on the Original Sin, central in Augustine, is a fresco preserved in the *Crypt of the Original Sin*, located a short distance from Matera.[90]

The crypt, with its Lombard-Benedictine style frescoes, is a testimony of priceless rock art. Around the 7th century AD, the territory of the Matera area was affected by a large flow of monks from the East, especially from the Holy Land. A detail of the narrative translated into fresco refers to the Original Sin:

> The fruit of original sin is represented as a fig tree and not as an apple, as notoriously indicated in scriptures or paintings. It is believed that the interpretation error is due to the incorrect translation of the Latin word pomum which can mean both apple and any other type of fruit. Very few other frescoes scattered around the world show the same particularity: among all, the scene of original sin depicted in the Sistine Chapel.[91]

---

90. IMAGE 8, p. 141

91. La Stampa newspaper (Turismo.it), *Matera, i Segreti della Cripta del Peccato Originale*, 20 April 2017; https://www.turismo.it/segreti-italia/articolo/art/matera-i-segreti-della-cripta-del-peccato-originale-id-14341/

The cult of images was not so immediate, due to the fear of idolatrous deviations inherited from the Jewish tradition, but until the Eighth century these tensions were limited and had no consequences for the Church as a whole. The society in which man lived, and in particular that of the first four centuries, was permeated at all levels by pagan practices and the risk of contamination was very present. Irenaeus cites the case of Carpocrates' Gnostic disciples: "they possess images, some painted, others made of different materials [...].

They crown these images and exhibit them with those of profane philosophers [...] They render these images all the other honors used by the pagans".[92]

Guided by the same fear, canon 36 of the Council of Elvira (300-303) states: "It seemed good to us to establish that in churches there should be no paintings, so that what is honored and adored is not painted on the walls".[93]

Instead, the patriarch Cyril of Alexandria expressed himself thus in defense of the images:

> Since the characteristics and prerogatives of divinity are difficult to describe and explain and they are denied observation, what could be said about them would prove to be completely insignificant and would remain beyond the truth. It is through the figures and images, as expressive as possible, as in a mirror or thanks to some arcane symbolism, that we learn to know them.[94]

---

92. BAUDRY, G.H. *Simboli cristiani delle origini*, p. 14

93. SENDLER, E. *L'icona immagine dell'invisibile*, 22

94. BAUDRY, G.H. *Simboli cristiani delle origini*, p. 14

7.3 Outbreak of the Crisis and Resolution

The iconoclastic crisis broke out following the *Quinisext Council* or "Council in Trullo", probably called in 691 by Emperor Justinian II. The intention was to address the need to follow up on the acts of the two previous councils that spoke out against Monophysitism, Origenism, Manichaeism, and against the remains of paganism, with the aim to reform customs in the Church and in Byzantine society.

Canon 82 proved to be of great importance for Christian iconography. In particular, for our purposes:

> In certain reproductions of sacred images, the Forerunner is depicted while showing the Lamb with his finger. This representation had been adopted as a symbol of grace, but it was a hidden figure of the true Lamb who is Christ our God, who was shown to us according to the law. Therefore, having collected these ancient figures and these shadows as symbols of truth, transmitted to the Church, we today prefer grace and truth themselves, as a fulfillment of the law. Consequently, in order to expose to all eyes, even with the help of painting, what is perfect, we decide that in the future we must represent Christ our God in his human form instead of that of the ancient Lamb.[95]

In this canon the symbol must give way to the face of the incarnate God, to the historical person of Jesus and, by doing this, it reflects for the first time the teaching of the Church on the icon, giving the possibility of expressing the reflection of the divine glory: another reality, spiritual and eschatological, is revealed through a historical reality.

This canon was accepted only a century later by Hadrian I because the crisis of the Byzantine empire – not only a religious one – broke out violently.

What is striking, in examining the events that occurred in those two centuries of history, is that the "salvation" of the icons was decreed by the hand of two very different women: Irene and Theodora.

---

95. SENDLER, E. *L'icona immagine dell'invisibile*, 22.

Both ascended to the throne following the death of their respective husbands, Emperor Constantine V in 780 and Emperor Theophilus in 842: bloodthirsty iconoclasts. The wives persevered in the veneration of icons, secretly while their husbands were still alive, openly after their death, when they succeeded them on the throne.

Originally from Athens, Irene – famous for having convened, together with Pope Adrian I, the second council of Nicaea (787) which deliberated in favor of images – also became sadly unpopular for cruelty: she blinded her son, an iconoclast, because she was no longer able to maintain control over him; a relationship hitherto characterized by suffocating protection. The coronation of Charlemagne in 800 decreed her end because, in addition to having had personal confictual relations with the future emperor (she arbitrarily broke off the engagement between her son, Constantine VI, and Charlemagne's daughter), the French court, not having even become aware of the convocation of the Council of Nicaea II, replied with her theologians to the council with the *Libri Carolini (Charles books)*, whose theses were confirmed by the Council of Frankfurt (794). In their view, the images were nothing more than a book for those who cannot read.

"They did not perceive with the acuteness of the Byzantines all the Christological dimensions of the icon, because they did not have to fight against monophysitism or against Islamic influences". The Greeks, in the eyes of Carolingian theologians, placed non-comparable values on the same level: "Man can be saved without seeing the images, but he cannot be saved without the knowledge of God".[96]

The coronation of Charlemagne was therefore perceived as a true usurpation of Byzantine law.

Particularly fascinating is the figure of the empress Theodora, first of all because during her reign (843-867?) Orthodoxy marked the definitive victory. Perhaps the time was ripe for this to happen.

---

96. Ibid., p. 32

However it may be, this great woman, as she has come to us, contributed to assigning equal dignity to icons with respect to and alongside the Sacred Scriptures. At court, everyone knew that with the passing of power into her hands she would impose the reestablishment of orthodoxy, since her great veneration for icons kept secret from the emperor was known in her circle. Theodora, however, did not want to hastily restore it; first of all, she had to make sure that the memory of her deceased husband was not clouded by anathema, for which she asked for and obtained the assurance of the Fathers that he would find grace before God. She wanted to overcome the opposition of the army and of a certain clergy, and to do this she decided to depose the patriarch John, choosing for this office the hegumen (abbot) Methodius, confessor of orthodoxy and much appreciated in Constantinople.[97]

Only after a year of preparations Theodora was ready to convene the council, where the canons of the first seven were proclaimed again, the cult of icons was declared legitimate and iconoclasts condemned as heretics.

The great victory of Orthodoxy was to be celebrated as a great event: on 11 March 843, the first Sunday of Lent, a solemn procession headed towards St. Sophia to celebrate the definitive triumph of truth. It was presided over by the patriarch Methodius, led by the Empress, accompanied by the whole court and followed by monks and faithful, many of whom still bearing the signs of their loyalty on the body. Each one carried an icon in procession.

Troparion 6 of the Matins canon:

> We keep the laws of the Church, laws observed by our Fathers; we paint the images; I worship them with the mouth, with the heart, with the will, those of Christ and those of the saints. The honor and veneration addressed to the image go back to the prototype: it is the doctrine of the Fathers, inspired by God, that we follow; and we say with faith to Christ: Bless the Lord, you that are all his works.[98]

---

97. Ibid., p. 36
98. Ibid., p. 36

Chapter Eight

THE THEORIES OF THE IMAGE

8.1 The Theories of the Image. East and West

Word and image must be closely related. We can translate every image into a word and for every word there is a corresponding image, at least in our mind. I am an absolutely human reality, belonging to the sensitive world. The same is true for any discourse you want to try about God, whether you approach him from the point of view of the Word or the Image: "It is not a question of juxtaposing word and image. The goal is the life-giving unity of the Word-Image. That is, the image says the Word, and the Word shows the image. Our path [as Christians] is therefore a Word that is a spiritual Image "and the spiritual image, so as not to confuse it, has been given a name: Icon.[99] The image falls into the category of signs, the Icon of symbols.[100]

Thought must correspond to reality and it is with signs that the human being represents the world to himself. On this truth the philosophers, from Plato onwards, have built different systems that have gradually formed two great currents of thought, Platonism and Aristotelianism: they determined the two different theories of the image, one followed in the East and the other in the West (culture and territory always determine a different way of feeling and conceiving reality, also extended to the Sacred).

---

99. PICCOLO, G.; SEBASTIANI, M. *La devozione popolare tra Arte e Teologia. Idolo e Icona*, (ed. Giuseppina De Simone), Nuova Serie Quaderni di arte e teologia, 2019 (ŠPIDLIK, T.; RUPNIK, M.I. *Parola e immagine*, p. 82)

100. SENDLER, E. *L'icona immagine dell'invisibile*, 75

8.2 Image as Participation in the Divine

According to Platonism, man recognizes things existing in the world because he has already encountered them in the Hyperuranium, the place where the corresponding ideas reside, and everything that exists in the material world is but a shadow of the eternal world of ideas.[101]

The theory that arises from here is "the image as participation in the divine".

John Damascene, in analyzing the different species of images, applies the Platonic categories of Dionysius the Areopagite.[102]

The image is ontological, not just poetic, participation (similarity) to the prototype: "A similarity that characterizes the prototype, while being different in something" and the degree of similarity depends on its participation or proximity to the prototype.[103]

It starts from the Word, a consubstantial image, to arrive at the icon as a "reflection of the visible realities in matter".[104]

---

101. "[Hyperuranium] none of the poets down here ever sang it, nor will they ever sing it in a worthy way. [...] In fact it is the being that really is, colourless and devoid of a figure and not visible, and that can be contemplated only by the pilot of the soul (intellect), and around which is found the genre of true knowledge, that occupies such place. [...]. [the soul] once it has contemplated all beings that truly are [ideas] and is satisfied with them, again enters the sky, and returns home". Cit., PLATO, *Phaedrus*, 247 c-e.

102. SENDLER, E. *L'icona immagine dell'invisibile*, 77, (DAMASCENE, G. *Adversus eos qui sacras imagines abiciunt*)

103. DAMASCENE, J. *Adversus eos qui sacras imagines abiciunt*, op. cit., PG94, 1240

104. SENDLER, E. *L'icona immagine dell'invisibile*, p. 77

It does so through the five images of different degrees of similarity.

1. The first image, the only one to be perfect, is the SS. Trinity. The Son is perfect participation with the Father; His nature is perfectly identified with the nature of the prototype.

2. The next degree of participation is the image that God has of the things created by Him, eternally present in His mind even before their existence.

3. The third kind of images are the visible things used by man to represent invisible things "without figure, so that, by depicting them bodily, we have a veiled knowledge of them".[105]

4. The fourth degree of imagery concerns future prefigurations, just as the burning bush evokes the Mother of God.

5. Finally the fifth genus, icons, since they evoke past things of which memory must be kept. Images expressed in the books with the word or reproduced on the paintings to be contemplated. "Thanks to them, we avoid evil and aspire to good. [...] We too, today, paint images (icons) of those who have been imminent in virtue, to recall them to our memory, to imitate them and for the love we bring them".[106]

The image occupies the lowest rung because the analogy is less perfect in its ontological participation. John Damascene had to answer for the material, "bad" for iconoclasm, therefore unable to represent spiritual realities. It is to rehabilitate it that he refers to the categories of Dionysius, basing the matter on Christology:

> I will not cease to venerate the matter for which salvation has come to me, but I do not worship it as God. How could God be what has had existence out of nothing? Even if the body of God is God, having become through hypsotic

---

[105]. Ibid., p. 78

[106]. DAMASCENE, J. *Adversus eos qui sacras imagines abiciunt*, op. cit., PG94, 1240

union without change that which gives the anointing, while remaining what it is by nature, that is, flesh harvested from a reasonable soul, created and not created? But I also venerate the rest of the matter through which salvation came to me, as if filled with divine energy and grace [...] I do not despise matter: it is not dishonorable, because nothing of what God has done is dishonorable.[107]

Therefore, the result is a well-deserved last step: all matter has been sanctified, it has received the divine breath through the body of Christ and from the latter to his effigy. The icon thus becomes a mediator of grace, like the Word when you do something, the Book: both signs that indicate the way; the Divine to be sought is expressed in the metaphor, the way in which man is best allowed to speak of God.

---

107. Ibid., PG94, 1245

8.3 Image as a Sign

The image that arises from the Aristotelian setting is "the image as a sign".

Man can know reality in two ways: through direct or indirect thought. In the first case, thought occurs without the need for intermediation with perception; in the second case, that of indirect thought, a sign is interposed between reality and spirit.

The relationship "means", implies a correlation between the signifier – an expression that can be sound or visual – and the meaning – a conceptual content of the signifier – put, in fact, in relation by the interpretant, who lives that specific context, since each sign acquires meaning only in its own "form of life".

In the sign, the spiritual world joins the material world and can be a representation adequate to reality, making the object present as a stylized copy or based on conventions, remaining in its domain closed in on itself, inherent (words or road signs are an example), or the sign can indicate an absent reality, an abstract sense. The meaning is no longer representable, here, and a dimension appears that goes beyond the signifier, now open to the infinite; it tends towards the unspeakable and becomes an epiphany. The symbol appears. The sign becomes a symbol, meaning and significant must come together in analogy.[108]

The sacred image retains all the properties of the sign and symbol, adding the human element. Early Christian thought makes extensive use of symbols, initially recurring to pagan ones that well represent the transcendent values of humanity. Enriched by a specifically Christian meaning, the original meaning will then give way to Christology and the Good Shepherd; an ancient image, will become Christ coming down the mountain to retrieve one of his lost sheep.[109] [110]

---

108. PICCOLO, G. *Fatti di parole*, pp. 106-107, 114-130
109. LUKE, 18,12. *Parable of the lost sheep.*

These two analyses, which at first sight seem distant, coincide. The analysis of the sign starts from the simplest form to rise up to the symbol with its epiphanic character, while the analysis of the image as participation in the divine proceeds in reverse, from the consubstantial image in the divinity to the icon. Both recognize in the latter the presence of the unspeakable springing from the material and the same literary sources apply to both: Sacred Scripture, the apocryphals, liturgical and hagiographic texts, and the sermons of the Fathers.

However, the Byzantine icons still retain their own artistic specificity, different from Western sacred art, the latter conditioned by the perspective and light studies of the late Middle Ages and the Renaissance.

---

110. In the chapter *The Divine Shepherd*, Dulaey explores the ancient sentiment that binds the shepherd to his sheep, asserting that in agricultural societies he is the image of cosmic harmony and happiness, since agricultural and pastoral civilizations. In the urbanized Greco-Roman world, where Christianity developed, the life of the shepherds became the image of the heavenly life of the dead in the afterlife and was recognized by the numerous sarcophagi decorated with pastoral scenes. In the Protestant Churches the heads of the communities are called "shepherds" and in the Catholic Church, bishops and abbots have as their distinguishing sign a stick, the pastoral, with a curved tip. In the parable of the lost sheep meanings are concentrated: the descent of the mountain, indicating the descent into hell but also the coming of the Son of God among men, and the divine Kenosis with which the divinity renounces all his omnipotence to become incarnate; the still waters of psalm 23 in the baptismal font; the nourishing herb of the Sacred Scriptures and the overflowing chalice, depicting the Eucharist that the neophytes received for the first time after leaving the baptistery. Furthermore, the image of the sheep on Christ's shoulders is confused with that of Christ on the cross: "The shoulders of Christ are the arms of the cross; it is there that I laid my sins, it is on the noble neck of that gallows that I rested. [...] Put the tired sheep, oh good shepherd, on your shoulders, that is, on the cross". Cit. St. Ambrose; On the *Gospel of Luke* 7, 209. On the psalm 118, 20, 33. With an accompanying ascent: salvation. See: DULAEY, M. *I simboli cristiani. Catechesi e Bibbia (I-IV secolo)*, Edizioni San Paolo, 2004, pp. 52-69

Chapter Nine
The Byzantine Icon

9.1 The Canon of the Icon

Despite their slow evolution, the canons of the Byzantine icon strictly observe tradition and it is easy, admiring them, to return to the origins. In my opinion, there is correspondence with the cult: in participating in an Orthodox Mass of worship one has the idea of being in the wake of Empress Theodora in procession to St. Sophia. The ritual is archaic, as are the melodies and sung psalms, enriched by ancient splendor, and the Archimandrite carries the icon of Theotókos in procession inside the basilica. At the end of the ceremony, the officiant invites the faithful to a banquet in rooms specially dedicated to this meeting between friends: cardamom coffee, biscuits and bread are offered to the Community, the same one that was consecrated shortly before and assumed in the Eucharist as the Body of Christ. Spending time in the inner courtyard of *Santa Maria in Cosmedin*, sipping coffee, continuing to eat that bread while getting to know people from the Mediterranean area, as well as from the Middle East, causes a very strong sensation: it seems to take a leap in time of two thousand years to land among the first Christians. We all recognize each other, even if we don't speak the same language.

One experiences the same feeling in front of Byzantine-style icons, whose canons are strictly transmitted mostly orally, although there is no lack of manuals. Among others, the manual sacred art of the monks of Mount Athos stands out: the Canon of the icon. The monks refer to the treatise of Dionisio da Furnà, an Athonite monk who lived there between 1701 and 1733, a period to which the drafting, found in 1839 in the Monastery of Esphigménou,, on Mount Athos by an archaeologist, presumably dates back. The legend built around this manual wants to derive the original draft from the mid-fifteenth century, based on a manuscript to be backdated by a few centuries.

The claim of tracing the manuscript back to the days of the iconoclastic dispute, or of being a code of Byzantine art, is rejected by studies already started during the nineteenth century. However, it remains a manual that came out of the practice of the laboratory:

Typos faithfully repeated for centuries in those isolated monasteries, beyond any rule dictated by time.

It begins with an invocation to the Mother of God, a brief appeal to painters eager to learn; a first part is dedicated to technology and the remaining five parts address each iconographic type, by describing in detail how to represent the corresponding Word. Thus, for example, the fourth part, entitled "Symbolic" and dedicated to the Parables. Here below, one at random:

> 25. The parable of the rich and poor Lazarus. There was a rich man, and he was dressed, etc. (Lk 16,19-31). It looks like this. A palace, and in it a table with various foods, and a man wearing splendid clothes sitting at it with a glass in his hand, and many servants serving him and bringing various foods, and further away again himself on the bed, and demons who drag out his soul and around him weeping women and children, and below the palace doors a naked and wounded man lying on the ground, dogs licking his wounds, and above him David with the harp and angelic hosts receiving his soul with trumpets and instruments, and farther away Hell, and the rich man in it who burns and says: Father Abraham, have mercy on me; and in front of him there is Paradise and in the midst of Abraham and in his bosom Lazarus, but Abraham replies to the rich man: Son, remember that you received your goods during your life; and the rest.[111]

The aforementioned representation falls within the literary genre of the epic model.

---

111. DA FURNÀ, D. *Canone dell'icona. Il manuale di arte sacra dei monaci del Monte Athos*, Pentàgora, Savona 2014, p. 172. IMAGE 9, p. 142

9.2 Literary Genres of Icons

The iconographer, it has been said, does not paint but writes an icon. The two terms, in Greek *gráphein* and in Russian *pisat'*, used to describe the work of the iconographer, expressing that this painting is similar if not identical to writing: it is a theology through images. Like any other type of story, it falls into a genre and the icon expresses itself through the literary genres of that era, conforming to their laws and schemes.

Konrad Onasch has identified four basic models: panegyric, epic, dramatic and dogmatic or theological.[112]

9.2.1 The Panegyric Model

Dominating this model is the rhetorical element and it is a type of discourse that was used in ancient times to celebrate great personalities. This literary genre uses bombastic but also poetic terms, because they must move and, at the same time, push the faithful to action, by imitating the deeds of the person raised to the honors: first of the crowds then, with Christianity, of the altar. The pagan panegyric celebrates heroes while the Christian panegyric praises the silent manifestation of grace, the meek one who fills with unearthly light, making martyrs an image of death and victory over it, as in the Death and Resurrection of Christ.

The key that opens us to the knowledge of oriental holiness is precisely this similarity with the Redentor, from nativity to death: the *Vitae* of the saints follow the same typical scenes (topoi). The Nativity, Christ the child, the gift of performing miracles until death and the Ascension into heaven, are of Christ as of the Virgin and of all the saints whose glory we want to magnify; scenes always referring to the Gospel

---

112. SENDLER, E. *L'icona immagine dell'invisibile*, p. 66 (ONASCH, K. *Die Ikonenmalerei*, Koehler-Amelang, Lipsia 1968, pp. 151-191)

as to other Sacred sources mentioned above. All the inhospitable environments, such as the deserts or the icy forests of Northern Russia, even if described in the lives of the Saints, do not enter the landscapes of the icon because they are sanctified and made an earthly paradise, where even the beasts are attracted to the Saint and they live peacefully with him.[113]

Examples of panegyric model are the topoi of the Mother of God which, born in the East, then spread also in the West, changing their name but maintaining the production technique.

Associated with a liturgical expression: "God made your bosom vaster than the heavens", to welcome himself, the *Panaghia* (all Holy) *Platytera* is born (the widest of the heavens, literally "with the largest body").[114]

To be exact, it translates a text by the Father of the Church Saint Basil, according to which God created the body of Mary large enough to accommodate the Incarnate Christ.

---

113. Ibid., p. 68.
On this ideal image, the *Bestiaries* were born in Europe around the 11th Century. Here, fantastic species coexist together with real animals, equally perceived as really existing, such as the dragon, griffin, phoenix, etc., assimilated by allegorical meanings. These animal books speak of the various zoological species not so much to describe them objectively and still less to study them in a scientific way, but to draw moral and religious meanings from them. They are works that speak of animals to better speak of God, of Christ, of the Virgin, sometimes of the Saints, and above all of the Devil, of the Demons and of sinners. They want to transmit the truths of the faith to invite the faithful to amend themselves. The study of the *Bestiaries* belongs to the cultural history of those populations: never, in any culture, are animals so present as in the Middle Ages; in Preaching, in sculpture, in stories, such as *Le Roman* de Renard, proverbs, seals, coats of arms, and so on. Artists and illustrators chose to draw animals not in a realistic way, because it was more important what these animals were to represent. The animal was "thought symbolically". The panther thus becomes a Christological image: all animals are attracted by its heavenly smell. Only the dragon, a diabolical symbol, escapes from its sight. See: PASTOUREAU, M. *Bestiari del Medioevo*, Einaudi, Turin, 2010, p. 10. IMAGE 10, p. 143

114. IMAGE 11, p. 144

Mary is presented in the attitude of a person praying, with her arms raised, her gaze turned towards the observer. On her chest she wears a large circle, called *clypeus*, inside which the Emmanuel can be found: the young Christ with the face of an old man and his forehead so high that he can understand the Logos. It is also called *Blachernitissa*, according to the icon of this type venerated in particular in the church of the Blacherne district in Constantinople. In Russian it is translated with the term *Snamenie*, "manifestation", "epiphany". In the West it became the *Madonna del Segno*.[115]

> In the East, the Marian figures present themselves to us under three main aspects.[116] The *Hodigitria* (or patroness of wayfarers), standing with the Child on her left arm. This type will take place in statuary and western ivories. The *Nikopoia* (who brings victory) seated on a throne on rich cushions, with the Child seated on her knees, facing her: this is the version that had the greatest development in the Christian world. The *Blacherniütissa* (from the name of the church founded by St. Pulcheria), which corresponds to our praying one and from which derives, in the VIII century, the *Panagia Platytera*, praying Virgin with a *clypeus* on the chest that contains the image of the Savior (Cologne, church of St. Pantaleon; Venice, S. M. Mater Domini; Chio, Nea Moni, etc.). Eastern Marian iconography profoundly influenced the devotional figurations of the West but from the XIII century onwards it carries them out freely, while the Greek-Slavic-Byzantine world preserves in its icons, almost crystallized up to our times, the hieratic type of Mary.[117]

Our Lady of Perpetual Help derives from *Panaghia Strastnaia*.[118]

The iconographic theme underlines the participation of the Virgin in the Passion of Jesus. The Mother is depicted holding out her right hand to her Child. Jesus, in learning his destiny just revealed to him by the

---

115. HAMILTON, G. *The Art & Architecture of Russia*, Yale University Press, 1992

116. IMAGES 12 and 13, pp. 145-146 14 and 15, pp. 147-148; 16 and 17, pp. 149-150

117. See: http://www.treccani.it/enciclopedia/maria-vergine_%28Enciclopedia-Italiana%29

118. IMAGES 18 and 19, pp. 151-152

archangels Michael – pictured at the top right, in the act of supporting a vase from which emerge the spear and the reed with the sponge – and Gabriel, on the left – while he shows the cross and the nails –, is seized by a movement of fear, underlined by a shoe escaping from his foot.[119] He finds shelter and comfort in Maria's arms, as he squeezes her right hand with both little hands. The archangels have veiled hands, as a sign of adoration, as always happens in the presence of the Theophany.[120] They operate a double recognition: the God-made-man is present in the Child; the Passion and the Cross are the signs of the Resurrection and the redemption of all humanity, a concept expressed in the paschal mystery.[121]

This is the Madonna venerated in Fumone, the village where Celestine V, the "Pope of the great refusal", was imprisoned by his successor Pope Boniface VIII, for fear of a secession.

The biographical material on the Virgin is not provided merely by the *Gospel* but by parallel tales dated between the Second and Sixth centuries, which took the form of Apocryphal Gospels collected later, towards the end of 1200, in the so-called *Golden Legend*, by Jacopo da Varagine, Bishop of Genoa.[122]

---

119. See: https://immaculate.one/la-madonna-del-giorno-27-giugno-madonna-del-perpetuo-soccorso-chiesa-di-santalfonso-allesquilino-roma-italia#.XqgFCS1aYnU

120. See: https://iconemirabile.wordpress.com/2016/02/06/icona-della-madre-di-dio-della-passione/

121. See: http://www.santiebeati.it/dettaglio/20260

122. See: http://www.treccani.it/enciclopedia/maria_%28Enciclopedia-dell%27-Arte-Medievale%29/

9.2.2 The Epic Model

The emphasis of the epic model is on fidelity to history. It tells, in chronological order and in detail, biblical events and the lives of the saints.

There is a main image around which scenes develop, as in the case of some icons in the panegyric, but here in "continuous style", that is, within the icon and linked together without interruption.[123]

They mostly refer to the prophet Elijah, much venerated in Russia, who became protector of rural populations supplanting the pagan god Perun. The central part is always occupied by his assumption into heaven on a chariot of fire and around the scenes of his life, that led him to holiness.

The icon of the Nativity also follows the epic model: it sees in the manger and the Virgin in a black cave, a symbol of darkness, in which the Child shines, wrapped in white swaddling clothes (as white are His robes in the descent into Hell and Resurrection).[124] The crib becomes an altar to which Jews and Gentiles are invited to eat, represented respectively by the ox and the donkey.[125] The introduction of the two animals is based on St. Jerome and two prophetic texts: "The ox knows the owner and the donkey the master's crib, but Israel does not know and my people do not understand".[126] In the *Vulgate*, St. Jerome's version of the Latin Bible, we read: "he lay down between the ox and the donkey". From the VI to the XVI century, the Nativity will always be represented with these two animals.

---

123. SENDLER, E. *L'icona immagine dell'invisibile*, 68

124. IMAGE 20, p. 153

125. See: http://www.homolaicus.com/storia/medioevo/iconografia/93.htm

126. ISAIAH, 1,3. *Habakkuk*, 3,2

Below the two scenes from the *apocrypha*, St. Joseph in doubt and two midwives: one Salome and the other symbolically representing Eve, about to wash the child. Only later St. Joseph will be included in the Nativity scene.

> The epic model faithfully follows the tales of sacred books or hagiographers. However, the icon does not become a simple illustration of history, since its spiritualized forms give it an aura of mystery: it translates, in its own way, the supernatural dimension of Scripture and the life of the saints.[127]

9.2.3 The Dramatic Model

Already Aristotle, between 334 and 330 BC, in his treatise on Poetics, judged "tragic theatre, that is to say the most political, communal and dialogical of the poetic arts, superior to any other poetic genre". And from tragedy he captures, as its fundamental elements, the ability to stage the role of passions (of which tragedy is catharsis), the value and nature of *eudaimonia* and the value and nature of *philia*. Catharsis, happiness and friendship are for Aristotle the distinctive elements of the tragedy: "fundamental for deciding what is the good of human conditions".[128]

The dramatic element, far from being simply a theatrical technique, has a prominent place in all the arts, as well as in sermons and religious stories. Dramatic tension fascinates men and already, in the II century, Melitone Bishop of Sardi used it in his dialogues.

> 50. The misfortune of humanity on earth was frightening and unheard of. This is what their fate was. Sin will strike them 26. seized them and pushed them towards the waves of passions, where they were inundated by insatiable cults: adultery, fornication, impudence, greed, thirst for gold, murder, blood,

---

[127]. SENDLER, E. *L'icona immagine dell'invisibile*, p. 69

[128]. GUASTINI CARROCCI, D. *Poetica*, Rome, 2010, p. 26. (Text cited by PICCOLO, G. *Il gioco dei frammenti. Raccontare l'enigma dell'identità*, San Paolo, 2020, 84)

cruel tyranny, criminal tyranny. 51. The father brought the dagger against the son, the son raised his hands on the father, the wicked struck the breast that had suckled him, the brother killed his brother, the host wronged the host, the friend slaughtered the friend, the man slaughtered the man with the hand of a tyrant. 52. On earth they had all become those who homicide, who fratricide, who patricide, who infanticide. But something more monstrous and unheard of still was invented: a mother put her hands on the flesh she had generated, threw herself on the flesh she had fed with her breasts, swallowed the fruit of her bowels in her bowels and, the unfortunate mother, was transformed into a horrible grave, swallowing the child she had carried in her womb.[129]

The suffering of Christ's life, of his Passion and Resurrection, always evokes the drama of the Redemption: finally, an answer to the unsolvable suffering for the pagan world, but also for the Jews who do not recognize Christ as the Savior. The icon of the Cross, through the veiled opacity of death, renders the epiphany of the Son of Man: everything inspires calm and peace, the gestures of the characters are composed and express a painful compassion, portrayed in human and sacred dignity of earthly suffering.[130]

"Christ, the king of the universe", the exegetes of the early Middle Ages point out, "never laughed – the Gospels testify – and contented himself with weeping softly for the death of Lazarus, before the grievances of Martha and Mary convinced him to the sensational miracle of calling his friend back to life".[131]

---

129. MELITONE DI SARDI, *Sulla Pasqua*.
See: http://www.notedipastoralegiovanile.it/images/documenti/omelia%20sulla%20santa%20pasqua.pdf

130. The Cross preserves for us Catholics the same evocative and prayerful power assumed by the icon for Orthodoxy.

131. FRUGONI, C. *La voce delle immagini. Pillole iconografiche dal Medioevo*, Einaudi, Turin, 2010, p. 5

In those first centuries, the Church distanced itself from attitudes that flaunt pain, since they evoked the pagan modes of mourning, but above all because the Resurrection to new life makes death a rebirth in the Kingdom of Heaven. St. Ambrose thus underlines the demeanor of the Virgin: "Mary was standing near the cross of her Son and the Virgin contemplated the martyrdom of her only-begotten son. I read in the Gospel that she was erect, I do not read that she was crying".[132]

Thus the man of that time, faced with the figure of Mary with an expressionless face, who with one hand holds the wrist of the other – as in the wooden group "Christ crucified between Mary and St. John the Evangelist", in St. Peter's cathedral in Bologna – receiving in a gesture all the pain felt by the Virgin but also trust in returning to the Father.[133]

Making the pain blatantly manifest was only of the damned and here all the drama of the most touching theatrical tragedies comes into play: they do not preserve any dignity or attitude in showing the degradation that is no longer human and the tortures suffered. They exhibit in distorted and deformed faces while the demons translate their cruelty into images with terrifying grins and with a threatening aspect: they make tongues or obscene gestures, multiply their faces, cut, shred, skewer, and the chaos is strengthened by the turbulent movement of their straight hair or flaming eyes. They were supposed to terrify the "eternal prisoners", but above all this narrative genre had great educational power: the faithful who stood in front of the opera, as well as the spectator in the theatre, could recognize themselves without feeling judged. The tympanum of the Saint-Lazare cathedral preserves a magnificent stone bas-relief sculpted in the XII century by

---

132. COPPA, G. *Sant'Ambrogio*, Opere Utet, Turin 1979, p. 832

On the character of the representation of pain in the early Middle Ages see FRUGONI, C. *La grammatica dei gesti, qualche riflessione*, in *Comunicare e significare nell'Alto Medioevo*, Atti della LII settimana di studio del Centro Italiano di Studi sull'Alto Medioevo, Cisam, Spoleto, 2005, vol. II, pp. 895-936

133. IMAGE 21, p. 155

Gisleberto. At the centre of the ranks of the damned who go to hell, two huge hands with hooked fingers emerge from nowhere and crush the weeping head of a sinner stained with pride. Central because the Fathers of the Church already defined it as the "root of all evils", rendered in an image by the damned subject whose hands rested on his thighs. Those hooked and slender fingers not bound to any body achieve the purpose of transmitting anguish. On the left we can distinguish the screaming miser while a snake attacks the bag containing the money of his perdition and, on the right of pride, the lustful woman bitten in the breasts by another snake, the hand of the sinner resting on her cheek to express mere pain and repentance, now belated.[134]

The "ugly", with a terrifying aspect, associated with the devil and the antichrist, enters the Christian world with the "Revelation" on the island of Patmos of St. John the Evangelist, translated in the *Apocalypse*, and with it the fear of the end enters the medieval imagination. In the Old and New Testament, we certainly speak of devil and hell, but the devil is named through the actions he performs or the effects he produces, except for the serpent form taken in the book of *Genesis*. St. Bonaventure, in his biblical "story", identifies the antichrist in multiple characters with different names and faces that animate the narrative: Lamech, who was the first to introduce bigamy; Nimrod, under whose authority Babel was built; Dan, the fraudulent who hides in the sand to grab his prey. He speaks of the seven-headed abyssal beast that rises from the abyss and tramples everything, commenting on the *Apocalypse*.[135] If read without any allegorical interpretation, it is comparable, citing Eco, to a "disaster movie", where no detail is spared, and this is how it inspired the artistic images of the centuries to come.[136] [137]

---

134. IMAGE 22, p. 156

135. SAN BONAVENTURA, *La sapienza cristiana. Collationes in Hexaëmeron*, Collatio XV, Jaca Book, p. 206-209

136. ECO, U. *Storia della bruttezza*, Bompiani, Milan, 2013, p. 73

137. IMAGE 23, p. 157

9.2.4 The Model of the Theological Treatise

Even the most modest icon implies a theological background; "the image represents what Scripture teaches with the word. Theology deepens a truth with reasoning; the image, instead, offers it as a vision: for this reason, the image always remains in the figurative field, even when it transfigures concrete reality to highlight the theological significance".[138]

While the panegyric genre remains the domain of language and form – making of the icon a *laudatio* to the Saint – "the theological element concerns the very essence, the represented object, whose mystery it reflects, thus elevating the Byzantine art at its last stage of spiritualisation".[139]

From the 16th century, in Russia, the icon is transformed and is no longer a hypostatic presence of the prototype but becomes a treatise on theology: a phenomenon that can be illustrated by following the evolution of the icon of the Holy Trinity.[140]

Philoxenía (hospitality) was the name by which it was known in the Byzantine world; a name already present in a IV century mosaic in Santa Maria Maggiore, where Abraham welcomes three visitors (the Most Holy Trinity, an episode reported in *Genesis*).[141]

The three characters have a theophany style while the details respect a historical conception (the care of the hosts, Sarah and Abraham, the objects on the table, the servant who sacrifices the calf).

---

138. SENDLER, E. *L'icona immagine dell'invisibile*, p. 71

139. Ibid., p. 71

140. IMAGES 24, 25, 26, pp. 158-159-160

141. *Genesis*, 18, 1-15

With Andrej Rublëv the composition is totally dominated by the dogmatic aspect and the details are reduced to the essential: the three people communicate with silent gestures; the table has been transformed into an altar with only the Eucharistic cup while the cliff, the oak, and the house, are transformed into symbols that hint at the painter's intention: "to represent the Trinity in its movement of love and as a cause of salvation for men. This conception does not diminish the historical value of the scene but superimposes a theological interpretation on it".[142]

Florensky puts it this way:

> It so happened that the historical particularities gradually fell by themselves from the composition of the image, and the icon of Rublëv, old and new together, proto-revealed and completely repeated, became a new canon and model, confirmed by the ecclesial conscience and reiterated in a normative way by the Council of Hundred Chapters [Stoglav] and by the other Russian Councils.[143]

The latest evolution of this icon sees the three figures proceeding from the Father to the Son to the Holy Spirit: a purely theological conception. In the *Icon of Paternity*, we observe the Father, seated on the Throne, carrying the Son on his knees (every time a character is found in someone's lap, he indicates sonship); Jesus carries in his hand a halo, in which the Holy Spirit is enclosed in the form of a dove. "The Son is in the bosom of the Father" and above all reflects the definition of Gregory Nazianzen, when he distinguishes the three persons and their relations: the Father is uncreated, the Son is born of the Father, the Spirit proceeds and is sent.[144]

---

142. SENDLER, E. *L'icona immagine dell'invisibile*, p. 72
143. FLORENSKIJ, P.A. *Le porte regali*, p. 51
144. JOHN, 1,18

The same dynamic conception of the mystery is also expressed in the canon of Pentecost:

King of Kings, One of the Only,
only Word that proceeds from the Father without beginning,
in your benevolence, you truly made your Spirit shine,
equal to You in power, on your apostles singing to you:
"Glory to your power, Lord".[145]

Egon Sendler considers this a sad evolution, since the essence of the icon was the image that covered the mystery, which first became pure doctrinal teaching, then a game of signs and symbols for the proud spirit of its subtleties. He also wonders how the icon could have lost its theological richness with its language and its means of expression, and how it could have succumbed to rationalism despite all its spiritual depth.

He hopes to find the true icon under his ever-new face: "the icon in which the values of our time are reflected, but even more the Christian faith of all time".[146]

---

145. SENDLER, E. *L'icona immagine dell'invisibile*, p. 72
146. Ibid., p. 73

Chapter Ten
Light and Perspective

10.1 The Icon Rejects the Real

"If I don't know exactly what a given sign means, well, it's free then to mean everything to me. In a sense, poetic joy and affective exaltation then only become wider, and more indeterminate".[147]

The Byzantine icon purposely comes out of any reference to reality, both from the perspective and from the likelihood of the light rendered.

In order for it to appear, it must somehow upset, get out of the ordinary vision and draw the viewer into the question: "Why is a child represented with an elderly face and a forehead so disproportionate as described in Emmanuel?". The Icons are filled with "whys" masterfully aroused, starting from the feeling of space.

---

147. PICCOLO, G. *Il gioco dei frammenti. Raccontare l'enigma dell'identità*, San Paolo, 2020, p. 36. (MARITAIN, J. *L'intuizione creativa nell'arte e nella poesia*, p. 288)

10.2 The Beautiful and the Sublime

The first point of division between Icon and Western Sacred art seems to be the search for the Beautiful and the Sublime, of vague Kantian reconstruction. The beauty, for Kant, concerns the form and expresses limitation, while the sublime is recognized in the absolutely great and it refers to the infinite: "The beauty of nature concerns the form of the object, which consists in limitation; the sublime, on the contrary, is also to be found in a formless object, provided that unlimitedness is represented in it, or occasioned by it [...]"; to this he adds the "totality of thought", always placing as a privileged point the *Dasein*, thus moving away from our icon.[148]

Following this first divergence, we could say with him that beauty is pursued in the Sacred Art of Western production: the tendency to objectivity, to a careful imitation of nature in reproducing subjects and objects through a scientific perspective, in often crowded and in any case not very intimate environments; all considerations that lead back to reality, with the result that that work could remain in the immanent sphere. Although the cycle of frescoes in Giotto's Scrovegni Chapel in Padua is beautiful, it firmly maintains the idea of "artfully constructed work" (if you want to say so): magnificent, but difficult to use in prayer. The Annunciation can be admired, and the features of the Angel appreciated: the enchantment of the Virgin's face, her posture as a humble handmaid sitting and with her arms crossed on her chest, to say "May His will be done". The room and the whole architectural structure that surrounds the characters follows the rationality of the real and the relationship with the divine promises but hardly lights up. She remains on the level of wonder, that awakened in front of the work of a great artist: she remains imprisoned in his hands and in his idea, in his masterful act of translating his intuition, his devotion to the Virgin translated into a visual image.[149]

---

148. KANT, I. *Critica della facoltà di giudizio*, p. 80

In the Sublime, everything tends towards infinity; the Beautiful results from contemplation that becomes transcendent, feelings overflow, ranging in the irrational, in the dimension of the dream, attracted there by the means of representation. In the Beautiful space is sensitive, in the Sublime there is the sensation of space.

> The face and the spiritual aspects of things are visible to those who have glimpsed in themselves the primeval face, the face of God, or, in Greek, the idea: enlightening, it sees the idea of Being herself and, through herself, what is revealed to the world; she sees this world of ours as an idea of the superior world. Thus, the images that separate the dream from reality, separate the visible from the invisible, and join the two worlds. In this frontier place of dream images, their relationship is established both with this world and with the other.[150]

However, Byzantine art has its own, well-defined, way of seeing and representing, while not observing the perspective patterns of Beauty. "The perspective, all considered, belongs to the field of technique, not to that of art", and acquires the symbolic form.[151]

K. Onasch recognizes only two perspective forms in Byzantine art: the perspective of importance and the epic perspective. The first one is recognized in the simple juxtaposition of several saints in an icon; the central character has larger dimensions while the others create the perspective space. The epic perspective has a narrative and theological character at the same time: there are no lines of flight but lines that make the theological sense of the scene appear so that the viewer can contemplate it through the things represented; things making the scene transparent.

The Byzantine icon gives the shape of an idea to reality and therefore the observation of nature is not needed for this purpose.

---

149. IMAGE 27, p. 161. I chose the Annunciation by Beato Angelico because it is even more dense with symbolic meanings.

150. FLORENSKIJ, P.A. *Le porte regali*, 20

151. SENDLER, E. *L'icona immagine dell'invisibile*, p. 137

P.A. Michelis, the author of *The Aesthetics of Byzantine Art*, sees the Byzantine perspective as a "reaction against the naturalistic and rationalist art of antiquity. The category of the sublime has taken the place of the beautiful and its irrationality has transformed the conception of space".[152]

[152.] Ibid., p. 139

10.3 Natural Light and Spiritual Light

Dionysius the Areopagite, the theologian and philosopher who most influenced medieval art, describes in his system how everything is determined by the irradiation of divine light towards creatures: "Through the icon the truths of faith radiate towards those who contemplate it. Thus, the movement that in the naturalistic painting leads towards the vanishing point is reversed, going towards the one who looks".[153]

The structures and laws of representation are therefore inverted, just as the laws of light, natural or spiritual. The light of the icon has nothing to do with natural light, because it is materialized grace received from contemplation.

Under the dome of Galla Placida in Ravenna, thousands of stars plunge the gaze into an endless depth, which attracts, almost lifts, the whole body towards the unfathomable and mysterious infinity. Depth that in the icon is provided by the gold background: "a uniform and infinite space like the sky that contains all things".[154] Gold in the halos, gold filigree on Christ's robes... Gold is found wherever you want to signal participation in the life of God and on everything that is royal and sacred (it is also found on the imperial documents of Byzantium). The gold shading (*assistka*) is only in the icon. In any other pictorial genre, the use of gold makes an "abominable impression and the gold paint is on the painting like a gilded piece casually stuck to the surface, which one almost wants to erase".[155]

In the Slavic manuals of iconography, the gold background is simply called *svet*: light.

---

[153]. Ibid., p. 140

[154]. Ibid., p. 136

[155]. FLORENSKIJ, P.A. *Le porte regali*, p. 78

From the Renaissance onwards, we are used to seeing images in Western painting take shape through contrasts of light and shadow that make an illusion of reality, an illusion that is absent in the icon: "There is no *one* source of light: image and light are not separate. The light is inherent, it radiates directly towards the viewer", not to dazzle him but to reveal Beauty.[156]

"Now the powers of the heavens with us invisibly give worship. Here, in fact, the King of glory enters", at our side in worship, and the Glory of God is present in the icon: this Other presence is touched, kissed, venerated, but it is not the matter that is honored; that piece of wood, those colours, shapes, everything becomes transparent to give way to Glory. And the Face appears.[157]

---

156. Ibid., p.162

157. Hymn to the Offertory for the Byzantine Liturgy of Gifts presented in Great Lent.

Conclusions

Psalm 42 (41) - Lament of the Exiled Levite

[1] To the choirmaster. Maskil. Of the sons of Kore.

[2] As the hart panteth after the water brooks, so panteth my soul after thee, O God.

[3] My soul thirsteth for God, for the living God: when shall I come and appear before God?

[4] My tears have been my meat day and night, while they continually say unto me: Where is thy God?

[5] When I remember these things, I pour out my soul in me: for I had gone with the multitude, I went with them to the house of God, with the voice of joy and praise, with a multitude that kept holyday.

[6] Why art thou cast down, O my soul? and why art thou disquieted in me? hope thou in God: for I shall yet praise him for the help of his countenance.

[7] O my God, my soul is cast down within me: therefore, will I remember thee from the land of Jordan, and of the Hermonites, from the hill Mizar.

[8] Deep calleth unto deep at the noise of thy waterspouts: all thy waves and thy billows are gone over me.

[9] Yet the LORD will command his loving kindness in the daytime, and in the night his song shall be with me, and my prayer unto the God of my life.

[10] I will say unto God my rock. Why hast thou forgotten me? why go I mourning because of the oppression of the enemy?

[11] As with a sword in my bones, mine enemies reproach me; while they say daily unto me. Where is thy God?

[12] Why art thou cast down, O my soul? and why art thou disquieted within me? hope thou in God: for I shall yet praise him, who is the health of my countenance, and my God.

In this mutual eternal search between God and man, the icon is for the Christians of the Eastern Church the bridge over the Abyss that calls the abyss, between the Father, source of life, and man, where "death is planted like a splinter in the heart of existence".[158]

Condemning all totalitarianism, in *Christianity and Democracy* Jacques Maritain devotes an entire chapter to the "Communist Problem".[159] This ideology presented itself as a doctrine, not just an economic system as it was for the first Christian communities: communism was a philosophy of life aimed at materialism and based on the absolute rejection of divine transcendence.

Trying to "destroy them by force, machine-guns and concentration camps, and invoke demons of triumphant German Racism, the Pagan Empyre and Fascism against them" is not, however, a viable solution for Maritain.[160] Communists are not communism and the effort of a good Christian will be aimed at alleviating the human unease that every tyranny inevitably brings with it.

"Reach out", speak from the heart, with love and generosity, making sure that the Face of Christ, so present since the beginning in that people, returns to warm their homes. "History has launched us in an apocalypse where we are no longer permitted to shut our ears to the Gospel"; only love for the individual, respect for the soul and freedom lived in a healthy democracy, allow us to feel the song.[161]

---

158. EVDOKÌMOV, P.N. *L'Ortodossia*, p. 472 (Spidlìk, *Alcune considerazioni sulla teologia dell'icona*, in ID., Alle fonti dell'Europa, II, 141-148)

159. MARITAIN, J. *Christianity and Democracy*, Charles Scribner's Sons, New York, 1950. *Christianity and Democracy* was published after the war was over, a war that saw Maritain unable to return to his homeland, having married a Jewish woman of Russian origin. From Toronto, where he taught at the Pontifical Institute for Medieval Studies, he harshly condemned the Vichì government in power in his homeland. All totalitarianism is for Maritain to be condemned: Christianity rests in Democracy.

160. Ibid., p. 84

161. Ibid., p. 88

Some time ago an Orthodox friend of Russian origins gave me a book as a gift: *The way of a pilgrim*, written by an Anonymous Russian. It is the story of a pilgrim set between 1860 and 1865 – the probable date of his death – in a Russia where travellers were housed in homes, and parishes, and wherever the Word of God incarnate was followed. The pilgrim left his homeland, taking with him the Bible received as a gift from his grandfather and a little dry bread: he wanted to assume the "Continuous Prayer", that of the "Heart"; he had to understand how His name could enter his limbs till taking possession of his breath. "Lord Jesus Christ / have mercy on me".[162] He found the *Philokalia*.

Interviewed, to the question "What can Orthodoxy give?" orthodox theologian Olivier Clément replied:

> I would like to say that Orthodoxy is beauty... *philokalia* means love for beauty. The genius of Orthodoxy is then a philocalic genius. This is what is most striking when you get to know the Orthodox Church for the best it can offer: the beauty of the liturgy, icons and music.[163]

Although Soviet communism tried by all means to eliminate God from the lives of the communists, it never succeeded. It could not succeed: the essence of Russian people is Christian, starting from the spoken language, Cyrillic, from the Holy Cyril who gave it shape. In their idiom there is no verb "to have" referring to people and things are not possessed as well as years. Therefore, to say "I have a house", one will say "with me there is (there exists) the house", and "I am not 50 years old" but "I have been given 50 years": the concepts of "existence" and "gift", so dear to Christianity. The English language, on the contrary, needs reinforcement: "it is not simply I have, but I have got", as the "theology

---

162. The "prayer of the heart" sung endlessly.
See: https://www.youtube.com/watch?v=AHP4Z84a_WY&feature=youtube&fbclid=IwAR3HvQQ2PECll7IAIAHdcuehd_wOXR-yZdmJDVLjWGkyc8YsXN2ARRG4icw

163. CLEMENT, O. *Memorie di speranza. Intervista di Jean-Claude Noyer*, tr. it., Jaca Book, Milan 2006, p. 182

of prosperity" proposes today.¹⁶⁴ The prototype of each Holy Icon is translated with *podlinnik*: authentic, true.

Every form of language, it was said, is closely linked to the culture in which it was born and developed, starting from the language itself, which bears it.

The icon has been lived by the Christians of the Latin Church for millennia in the same way, in the only true way in which we can relate, which is the Orthodox one, and in some places, in particular in Central-Southern Italy, it continues to be so, although faded from the specter of superstition. For too long, the "cultured" faith (that of theologians), and a "popular" faith (that of women with tears in their eyes, crying out "Long live Mary" when the icon carried in procession re-enters the church), have been kept distinct. The younger generations have thus preferred to remain on the sidelines and look absentmindedly, keeping their distance from those tears, also considered simple folklore by the Church of the learned.¹⁶⁵

The icon restores to man the "memory of original innocence and projects this memory into the eschatological and ineffable horizon of the world to come, where is the fulfillment of the action of the Spirit of the Lord (cf. 2 Cor 3:18)".¹⁶⁶

---

164. See: https://www.laciviltacattolica.it/articolo/teologia-della-prosperita-il-pericolo-di-un-vangelo-diverso/

165. I perfectly remember the first time I heard those cries and saw those tears: I was a little girl, and I came from Emilia Romagna to spend my holidays in Ciociaria, the land that was the birthplace of my father. They shook me deeply, frightened me, and I held my father's hand. He took me in his arms and there I realized that he too, silently, had his eyes moist from tears. He said nothing to me, I had never seen him cry and so I wanted to respect his silence. The next day he took me to church, introduced me to the icon of *Our Lady of Perpetual Help* and told me of the time that with his mother, my grandmother, knelt before her to ask that her father return unharmed from the war or to give grace for the food brought by the Romagna aunt on a truck driven by the Germans, who had made Fumone their headquarters.

The feeling of a Christian Europe was born around the year 1000 on the way to Santiago, in opposition on one side to Islamic Asia and on the other to the fearsome Vends, a Slavic population who practiced bloody rites in honor of Odin, the wisest of the gods. The demarcation to the north was marked by the flourishing city of Magdeburg, placed by Charlemagne – the Frankish king anointed by Christ – as a border between us Christians and the demonic Vends: inside, trees were cut down to build houses, roads and squares gathered around a church; beyond the walls of the city the idols hung from the branches of the trees of the forest-sanctuary inhabited by those peoples. They were described with vacant eyes and covered with iron mesh armor stolen from the Christian knights taken prisoner and also hung from sacred branches. The blood of the still dying victims was sprinkled over the runes to propitiate their favors, gaining the wisdom of their god in exchange, and those who ate the throbbing hearts of the unfortunates were assured power over the dead.[167] Stories from the first millennium.

For the definitive demarcation to the South, Europe will have to wait for the *Reconquista* of the Muslim Moorish kingdoms that included a large part of the Iberian Peninsula. A period that lasted almost eight hundred years (711-1492), which culminated on January 2, 1492 when the spouses Ferdinand of Aragon and Isabella of Castile drove Boabdil of Granada, the last of the Muslim rulers, into the Mediterranean.[168]

Paradoxically, "by forcing our continent to defend itself and to seek ways and means for a unitary action [the Saracen and barbarian incursions], have also induced it, in perspective, to better define itself in front of the *Other*".[169]

---

166. MIRRI, L. *Icona la bellezza rivelata. Suggestioni teologiche dell'icona*, Biblioteca Francescana, Milan, 2015, p. 25

167. HOLLAND, T. *Millennium. Re, predoni, cavalieri e la nascita della cristianità*, il Saggiatore, Milan, 2013, p. 77

168. IMAGE 28, p. 163

169. CARDINI, F. *Europa e Islam, storia di un malinteso*, Laterza, Bari, 2010, p. 12

But it is in the Mediterranean that our civilization has taken shape; if we closed our eyes and reopened them immersed in the middle of its waters, we would seem to be in a large lake: that of Tiberias.[170]

The Mediterranean has no predefined borders. Ancient wisdom suggested that our sea reaches as far as the olive tree grows but this is not the case everywhere:

> Its borders are neither defined in space nor in time. We do not know how to determine them and how. They are irreducible to sovereignty or to history, they are neither state nor national: they resemble the chalk circle that continues to be described and erased, that waves and winds, enterprises and inspirations enlarge or shrink. Along the coasts of this sea passed the silk road, the paths of salt and spices, of oils and perfumes, of amber and ornaments, of tools and weapons, of wisdom and knowledge, of art and science. The Hellenic emporiums were both markets and embassies. Power and civilization spread along the Roman roads. Prophets and religions have come from Asia. Europe was conceived on the Mediterranean [...] No smaller meters are suitable for the Mediterranean than its own. We betray it by approaching it from Eurocentric points of view, which consider it exclusively as a Latin, Roman or Romance creation, observing it from a pan-Hellenic, pan-Arab or pan-Zionist point of view, judging it from the position of any particularism, ethnic, religious or politic. The Mediterranean has never been just Europe – it has been much more for a long time, just as it has perhaps become less for some time – but they cannot be one without the other.[171]

The borders of the Mediterranean seem to me to rest in the great house of Abraham, so hospitable. Considered the progenitor of the Jewish people, by his sons Isaac and Ishmael the great descendency promised by God took place: the Christian and the Muslim one. The story of Abraham is told in the book of *Genesis*, the first of the Hebrew Bible and the Christian Bible and taken from the Quran.[172] [173]

---

170. See: https://www.vaticannews.va/it/papa/news/2020-02/papa-francesco-bari-discorso-vescovi-mediterraneo.html

171. MATVEJEVIĆ, P. *Breviario mediterraneo*, Garzanti, Milan, 2006, pp. 18-19

172. *Genesis*, 12-25

> Then the Lord appeared to him near the great trees of Mamre... He looked up and saw three men standing near him. As soon as he saw them, he ran to meet them from the entrance of the tent and bowed low to the ground ... He took butter and milk and the calf which he had prepared and set it before them, and he stood by them under the tree, and they ate.[174]

In the icon of Abraham's Hospitality – "the icon of icons" – those three Persons represent the Holy Trinity, but "if I don't know what exactly a given sign means, it is free to signify everything for me."[175] [176]

Then, I could dream of the three Abrahamic religions sitting one day at the same table and weaving the rope together to ensure the boat finally returned to safe harbor. Certainly, a utopia; certainly, in contradiction with what the canons of the icon impose, and attributable to heresy:

> Figurative art is on the border of discursive narration, but without a clarity of narrative the symbol is transformed into allegory. This does not mean that an allegorizing symbol is irremediably abstract, detached from the conscience of the person who devised it, but its ability to encourage contemplation and to propitiate immediate access to meaning is grasped by a minority, and allegorizing symbols of the kind, in their deviation from a universal statute in contrast with the genuine symbols and the unanimous conciliar indications – and even more so if they are exalted in spite of those indications – they become easy sources of heresy, that is of exile and, to put it in the Latin sense, of sectarianism.[177]

---

173. *Sura*, XIV-XV, see: http://www.sufi.it/Corano/14.htm

In the Islamic tradition, Abraham is considered the example of the perfect monotheist, but his Jewish origin is denied. He is defined as a "friend of God" and has a specific mission: to be the ancestor of all prophets, including Mohammed.

174. *Genesis*, 18: 1-8

175. Thus defined by the "Council of a hundred chapters" (1551).

176. IMAGES 24, 25, 26, pp. 158-159-160

177. FLORENSKIJ, P.A. *Le porte regali*, p. 52

Saint Augustine would have reproached me, here. I would then have had the desire to explain myself better and I would have thought of replying that Christianity, in the West, is no longer an experience. A tradition remains, for some an ideology, but not that experience he lived of the encounter with the Master in that private space where only He speaks, and we as good disciples listen and we turn to him to ask him questions in complete abandonment and trust; very few people are able to experience it, as if it were no longer so important. It seems that the man of the present no longer knows what to ask for.[178]

I would say, to our Saint, that that intimate place where the encounter with the Beauty of Truth is possible scares us, and self-deception is preferred to save us from us without His help. Then the Word is true and beautiful to the extent that it becomes true and beautiful for us, and the many interpretations that St. Bonaventure believed were necessary – because Sacred Scripture must be able to speak to everyone – are confused with the needs of each one. Need has supplanted desire, and it is in need that Beauty is sought. Consumerism, the "only begotten" child of capitalism, then acquires the status of religion, making it a cult that globalization seems to have made totalizing.

Consumerism is practiced. Faith no longer.

In Bhutan, that small state closed between the two giants China and India, it seems that they have noticed it and have therefore changed their point of reference: they no longer chase Gross Domestic Product,

---

178. AUGUSTINE, *Il maestro e la parola*, pp. 155, 167, 169

"Now, for all the things we know, we do not turn to those who speak with a voice that resonates from outside, but to the truth that internally presides over the same mind, perhaps invited to do so by words. And the one to whom one turns to teaches, the one who is said to dwell in the interior man, Christ, that is, the immutable power of God and the eternal Wisdom, to whom every rational soul turns to it, but who reveals himself to each one only through how much it can contain according to its own bad will or good will".

but GIH, Gross Internal Happiness, since Happiness cannot depend on gain, ever; already Aristotle, in the Nicomachean Ethics, warned us against this confused way of placing ourselves before the end. Beauty and Happiness are inseparable.

It is in this need to rediscover the experience lived in prayer, in relationships, that in my opinion the icon returns to show all its power; the icon is practical, it means action. It suggests to man that his physical doing can, through it, transfer or join the "cosmic doing", to discover that we are not alone, thrown into the world.

In his *On Happiness*, Pierre Teilhard de Chardin argues that in the world life rises towards ever greater complexity and the effect of this complexing is to deepen the sense of one's being. It identifies three phases of our personalization:

- *Focus*: man acquires the condition of man in cultivating himself; therefore, being means first of all making oneself and finding oneself.

- *Decentralization*: when physically and biologically man, like everything that exists in nature, essentially reveals plurality. This phase corresponds to a mass phenomenon; we cannot progress to our extreme point without going out of ourselves by joining with others to develop, with this union, a surplus of consciousness. Love is the key word.

- *Joy*: The highest level of "super-centering" corresponds to the joy of the interminable; a profound, superior joy. "The explosive joy of a life that has finally found an interminable space to expand".[179] It is this joy that the icon makes us explore and helps us experience.

---

179. See: DE CHARDIN, P.T. *Sulla felicità*, op. cit.

What undermines and poisons our happiness is to feel the bottom so close: the suffering of separations and wear and tear, the anguish of the passing of time (and, for some, of the choices to be made), terror in the face of fragility of possessions, disappointment in reaching the end of what we are and what we love. The object that nourishes endless joy is inexhaustible, because it is confused with the fulfillment of the world around us; therefore, it escapes any threat of corruption and death. To reach the zone of great joys it is necessary to transfer the pole of our existence into the greatest of us and commit ourselves to doing the smallest of things greatly. The icon is a way that allows us to join the immense.

Christian mysticism has never ceased to push further and further away its perspectives of a personal God: not only creator but animator and totalizer of a single universe, that he brings back to himself through the interplay of all the forces that we group under the name of Evolution. The world rises upwards, until it is transfigured into a "hotbed of loving energy", where the icon leads us: we approach it, touch it, and at that precise moment it is she who takes us by the hand, lightly, as we like it.[180]

Since the Second Vatican Council the Church has conferred on popular religiosity, or *popular piety*, all the centrality it deserves: this is no longer seen as a folkloric form imbued with superstition.

> [Popular piety], if well oriented, [...] manifests a thirst for God that only the simple and the poor can recognize; it makes us capable of generosity and sacrifices to the point of heroism, when it comes to manifesting the faith; it involves an acute sense of the profound attributes of God: fatherhood, providence, loving and constant presence; it generates interior attitudes rarely observed elsewhere to the same degree: patience, sense of the cross in daily life, detachment, openness to others, devotion.[181]

---

180. Ibid.

181. POPE PAUL VI, *Esortazione Apostolica Evangelii nuntiandi*, 8 December 1975, in EV/5, 1643-1644

The adjective "popular" indicates that there is no Church of the learned and a Church that is lived, experienced through worship in the practices of popular piety. There is a Church that gathers the "people of God" and popular religiosity has become a "theological place":

> Popular religiosity is therefore not only a space for translation and elementary elaboration of the contents of the faith. It is a *theological place*, a *revelatory* space in which these same contents emerge immediately and in a peculiar way that has no equal.[182]

There is an absolute need for a return to the origins, in the places of memory, to regain possession of what is properly human: the dialogue that arises spontaneously in each one with the divine and the artists are able to express it in a simple, immediate way. Atavistic.

Our Popes, from the Second Vatican Council to date, have taken it up again bringing it to the fore:

"There still exists, also in this arid secularized world of ours, a prodigious capacity to express, beyond the authentic human, the religious, the divine, the Christian".[183]

"The world we live in needs beauty in order not to sink into despair. Beauty, like truth, is what infuses human hearts with joy, it is that precious fruit that resists the wear and tear of time, that unites generations and makes them communicate in admiration. And this thanks to your hands".[184]

"May your art contribute to the affirmation of an authentic beauty that, almost reverberating the Spirit of God, transfigures matter, opening souls to the sense of eternity".[185]

---

182. DE SIMONE, G. *La devozione popolare tra arte e teologia*, p. 9

183. POPE PAUL VI to the artists. Speech given on 23 June 1973 in the Sistine Chapel and addressed to the world of the arts, to re-weave a new alliance in the wake of a glorious past.

184. The Fathers of the Second Vatican Council to artists, 8 December 1965

185. SAINT JOHN PAUL II, *Letter to the artists*, 4 April 1999

"[...] the history of humanity is movement and ascension, it is inexhaustible tension towards fullness, towards ultimate happiness, towards a horizon that always exceeds the present as it passes through it".[186]

Pope Francis highlights the centrality of the symbolic dimension: it is the language that the people of God create to relate to the Creator, expressed in popular piety (always reaching out towards a devotional image or a relic) which is a "theological place". A place in which we are called to learn from the Spirit, capable of linking "the anthropological aspect and the theological dimension [...], human creativity and territory", guaranteeing the Faith a habitat and offering it languages as a "communicative medium".[187]

"God wants us to be a people". He does not distinguish between the learned and the ignorant. People![188]

The Latin Church has sometimes used too "scientific" language while the People of God ask for the poetry of the Spirit. The icon gives us back the lost experience. Beauty unites us to God and to our brothers of the Eastern Church, from whom we can learn in this and with whom it is possible to hope for a Church (if not reunited) on a united journey towards the Truth.

Hope. Memory.

---

186. POPE BENEDICT XVI, in his speech of 21 November 2009, re-edited the act of his predecessor Paul VI, again summoning three hundred artists of all types from all over the world to the Sistine Chapel.

187. DE SIMONE, G. *La devozione popolare tra arte e teologia*, p. 11

188. Pope FRANCIS in his homily at Casa Santa Marta, on Friday 14 February 2020, on family and love. Since the Second Vatican Council, emphasis has been placed on the dignity of popular religiosity, no longer understood as a form of ignorance and superstition but as a "revelatory space" in which the same contents expressed in Sacred Scripture emerge. For this reason, since then the expression "popular religiosity" has been replaced by the much preferred "popular piety", because it is in piety that the Christian most recognizes himself and it is in popular piety that the people of God reaches its purest (never simple) and ancestral union with the Sacred. See: DE SIMONE, G. *La devozione popolare tra arte e teologia*, pp. 9-11 and 31-33

The Word to Images

Image 1, ref. 11

William Holman Hunt; The Light of the World, 1853-1854. Keble College, Oxford.[189]

---

189. HUNT, W.H. *The Light of the World*, Keble College, Oxford, 1853-1854

Image 2, ref. 21

Andy Warhol, Campbell's Soup, screen printing.

In 1962 Warhol, using screen printing, created the advertising series "Campbell's Soup", an anonymous brand of canned soups that became the symbol of that artistic path called "Pop Art" and of which Andy Warhol is still considered the maximum exponent. The art of the consumer begins: Coca-Cola, understood as a symbol of those objects that break down the gap between rich and poor. A Coca-Cola can be afforded by anyone and, however enormous the power of purchase of a millionaire, his Coca-Cola will not be better than that of anyone else. Of very poor extraction, opening the pantry and finding it full was a source of joy for the master of "Pop Art". Campbells' represented for him the portrait of his mother: it reminded him of the lunch they ate together when he was a child.[190]

---

190. See: Exhibition catalogue, *Andy Warhol*, Brasini Wing, Vittoriano complex, Rome, 2019

Image 3, ref. 29

Philip Augustus expels the Jews from France, miniature, after 1321, Bruxelles, Bibliothèque Royale, ms 6931 (5), f. 265r.

The mystical drive generated by millenarianism leads to anarchy, rigorism and debauchery. A thirst for justice and banditry where, from the apocalyptic inspiration, only the taste for purifying violence is exercised to identify the vicars of Satan, the antichrist and first enemy of Christianity. The followers of the Apocalypse have succumbed to the charm of the Beast, causing rivers of blood to flow.[191] The Jew was the perfect antichrist and, from the first crusade of 1096, the distorting mirror of prejudice was often applied to the Jews in various forms of art: they were represented with deformed noses, often with dark skin or, in the Germanic context, a clearly visible colour "wheel" was painted on their clothes as a sign of recognition; a wheel that, in reality, they were forced to sew on themselves.[192]

---

191. ECO, U. *Storia della bruttezza*

192. FRUGONI, C. *La voce delle immagini*, p. 156

Image 4, ref. 33

Map of Bedolina;
Upper Paleolithic (40.000 - 10.000 b.C.)

In Bedolina, Valcamonica, there is the most beautiful example of petroglyphs discovered so far. The Map initially seemed to depict the surrounding environment; a more accurate study brought out a complex representation, where not only the Oglio river, the valley below, the livestock, the stocks, the wooden houses with sloping roofs find space, but also the cult of the dead, memory, and votive offerings to the gods to guarantee a good harvest, hope. It's the form of humanity in its essence: Memory and Hope. It tells of men, in the difficult transition from a society of hunter-gatherers to one of farmers-shepherds, and the engravings would seem a rudimentary form of prayer.

Thinking the Beyond is thinking about the Limit and the body is the first limit. Contemplation of the immensity of the sky has aroused in man of all times wonder, admiration, a sense of infinity, while at the same time instilling a certain dismay at his own condition, of impotence in the face of so much incomprehensible greatness. There are two conflicting feelings, attraction and fear, firmly intertwined. St. Thomas emphasizes the dual significance of the term "amazement": it can be understood as "stupendous" but also "stupid"; that is, one who is amazed to the point of not being able to react. The human being cannot and must not live his entire existence in fear: he is destined to go further and must give himself answers. To remain in the night, without looking for a light that can illuminate one's path, would be in contradiction with what distinguishes it from other earthly creatures: reason.

Philosophy takes its first steps from the existential questions that humanity, since the dawn of its days, asks itself by reflecting on what has already happened, and it is from the contemplation of the infinite that man starts the reflection of the self as a finite being; a creatural being, forming part of a plan infinitely greater than himself.

Myth and philosophy still travelled together. The first limit of the living being is the corporeal dimension, actualized within earthly boundaries. Therefore, soon the desire to represent oneself was born, to find a finite and known space within which to signify one's own existence. The objectification of things makes us discover how man then began to engrave maps on the rocks, the first timid attempt to overcome the fear of the unknown and the desire to circumscribe his own space in time that would mark his passage.

The global era has given us a world/environment so large that it makes any search for something that goes beyond and encompasses the whole, pointless: so much already can be reached through a "click"; Mr. Google gives us the gift of an absolutely immense world; so immense that a lifetime would not be enough to probe the virtual. What is, then, the use of the metaphysical?

It is from the awareness of the limit that humanity takes shape; and it is in its own limit that science proceeds.

Image 5, ref. 68

Minangkabau, Sumatra Island, Indonesia. Cosmogony as a representation of meaning

The Minangkabaus live on the island of Sumatra, Indonesia. Their myths are centered on a symbolic vision of the world where the earth (whose seas are contained by a crown of mountains), is supported by the horns of a buffalo (a sacred animal, as they consider it the founder of their first clan). If the animal is stung by insects, the earth starts shaking causing earthquakes and catastrophes. The buffalo stands on a large egg, the origin of the world. This curious building is supported by a large fish, swimming in a sea of which it is impossible to know the boundaries.

"If language and symbolism consist in *remaking reality*, there is no place in language in which this work appears more evident: when symbolism transgresses its acquired boundaries and conquers unknown lands, then we can see the potential of its ordinary context".[193]

---

193. PICCOLO, G. *Fatti di parole,* pp. 110-111

The pictorial image is used in the most archaic forms of life as in the most complex ones, because it makes the metaphor alive, unequivocally and without hesitation.

The mythos was closely linked to the logos; it tried to explain the world by narrating it and the word of the myth was incontrovertible because of divine origin: the poet speaks in the name of the Muses. We then moved on to the graphic representation of "worlds", which gave a great deal of space to the imagination of tribes and peoples, countless visions that ancient sages, shamans, men and women believed in.

The myth in the biblical account of creation (Genesis 1.1-2.3), shares the dialectical tension between chaos and the cosmos with the ancestral vision of the first cultures. It does not intend to give a rational explanation of phenomena and their causes; it wants to narrate, founding the good principles of the world in an a-temporal dimension. The time of myth is not historical time. Its strength lies in its ability to overcome chaos.

God does not occupy a physical space but a logical one!

Image 6, ref. 69

Allegory of the hill of Wisdom. Siena Cathedral. Pinturicchio, dating from around 1505.

Amazement: amazed or stupid. The search for meaning begins. Only two of the ten men who landed fortunately on the island overcome fear and disenchantment by facing the ascent. They leave vices and sins downstream: the snakes of envy, the weasel of fraud, the tortoise of sloth ... They have to reach the top to be able to seize the palm offered by Wisdom (Quiet) on the throne. Waiting for them are the philosophers Socrates, ready to hand them the palm of victory, and Crathes, who despises wealth by throwing a basket full of jewels into the sea.

This floor mosaic depicts Ricoeur's eighth study by image, in showing the "service that the metaphoric language can perform within the philosophical discourse".[194] The living metaphor.

---

[194]. Ibid., p. 107

Image 7, ref. 89

Caravaggio, Rest on the Flight into Egypt, 1596, detail. Doria Pamphilj Gallery, Rome.

"The genius of the Christian religion is that although its mysteries transcend our understanding, it has found a way, above all thanks to art, to translate them into universally understandable terms, in situations common to all [...]. The primordial image of Western art is that of a mother with her child".[195] What leaves you breathless in art is therefore the representation of human beings through their inner states, first of all the love perceived in the way Mary holds Jesus in her arms. It translates dreams and expectations that all mothers project on their newborn child. Every mother is seized by a deep love mixed with amazement in finally seeing for the first time that creature that she carried in her womb for nine months: it is always different from what she had imagined for so many nights. It seems to be the first will of that piece of her flesh to become autonomous, different and more from her. The act of finally visible individuation, at first only sweetly perceived as essence: that "actus essendi" of which Thomas speaks can be perceived from the first instant without any explanation; science does not speak of it. Then you raise your eyes to heaven and look for Mary, the Mother: only she can understand what you are feeling. Thus, one enters into a wonderful empathic relationship, which transcends reality, as is the relationship with the creature who has just become part of one's body and which still does not give obvious signs of its presence. There are moments of infinite joy and others of fear, she is beside you and makes sure that fear does not end in anguish: the place where Heidegger meets nothingness. The Mother with the Child on her knees excites and is the source of pure popular devotion. The Marian cult spread throughout the Christian world as early as the Council of Ephesus, summoned by Emperor Theodosius II in 431. The relationship between the Virgin and painting was captured by the tradition that sees Luke, the Evangelist of the Virgin, as a painter.

What Caravaggio writes on this canvas is a moment of rest that the Mother takes with her little one in her arms. Every mother has lived through these moments, the eyes of faith will see the sacredness of the characters in this painting only after having "internalized a complex metaphysical narrative, which begins with insubordination, sin and the knowledge of good and evil. [...] There is a difference between knowing that the Madonna and Child are happy and knowing that the Madonna is free from sin and has been chosen as a vehicle by the Holy Spirit".[196]

---

195. DANTO, A.C. *Che cos'è l'arte*, p. 68

196. Ibid., p. 69

Image 8, ref. 90

Matera; Crypt of the Original Sin.[197]

---

197. See: https://www.youtube.com/watch?v=KosLquviEB4

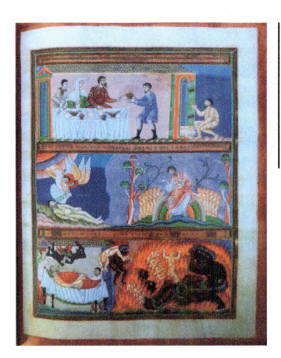

Image 9, ref. 111

Codex Aureus Epternacensis. Gospel of Echternach; 1030 approx.; Benedictine Abbey of Echternach; Client Abbot Humbert of Echterbach; Nuremberg, Germanisches Nationalmuseum, Hs. 156142.[198]

---

198. WALTER, I.F.; WOLF, N. *Capolavori della miniatura. I codici miniati più belli del mondo dal 400 al 1600,* Taschen, Colonia, 2003, p. 129

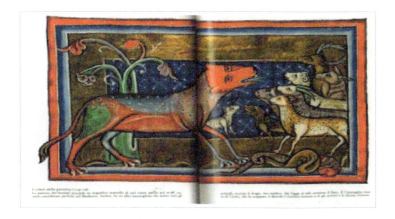

Image 10, ref. 113

The colours of the Panther; 1240 circa, Michel Pastoureau, Bestiaries of the Middle Ages, 10

The panther is a beast with wonderful properties in all respects, starting from the etymology of the name: it begins with pan which in Greek means "everything"; just like Christ for men, the panther in the animal world is the incarnation of a great unifying whole. Its fur is depicted in seven colors (a number considered perfect, at the time of the painting). The mantle can be sprinkled with rims, stars, crescents, many colored eyes and sometimes streaked or spotted. Its smell is sweet, all animals are attracted to it: it is the odor of sanctity, Heaven and Christ, to which it is compared. The beasts following the panther, when it comes out of the forest, are the kind men who followed the Savior after resurrection. The panther gives birth only once in her life because the little ones, eager to go out, hurt her belly. The teaching that was drawn from this was respect for parents and patience.[199]

---

199. PASTOREAU, M. *Bestiari del Medioevo*, Einaudi, Torino, 2010, p. 10

Image 11, ref. 114

Panaghia Playtera.[200]

---

200. See: http://www.latheotokos.it/modules.php?name=News&file= print&sid=1454

Image 12, ref. 116

Processional icon of Maria Odigitria among prophets, 1512-13, from Vallacchia

The Panaghia Odighitria, "She who indicates the way" (hodòs = via), takes this name from a church in Constantinople where the guides for the pilgrims' caravans met. She is shown standing with the Child on her left arm, while her right hand points to him and the child holds a scroll in the left. In the West, it became the fundamental type of Gothic Madonnas.[201]

---

201. Image: SAILKO, I., public domain

Image 13, ref. 116

Panaghia Nikopoia.[202]

The *Panaghia Nikopoia* "gives the victory". She sits majestically and sternly on the throne and holds the Child with both hands towards the observer, placing him before all. This is the typical attitude of the sovereign therefore it is also called *Kyriotissa* (Lady, Queen) in Russian. From this representation the enthroned Madonna was born in the West.[203]

---

202. Image: MYRABELLA, public domain
203. See: http://www.liturgiabizantina.it/icone/testi/theotokos_3.htm

Image 14, ref. 116

Panaghia Glykophilousa.

Panaghia Glykophilousa represents Mary in an affectionate attitude: the tender young mother who (literally) gently kisses God her Son.[204]

---

204. Image: ANDREW, public domain

Image 15, ref. 116

Eleusa.[205]

The *Panaghia Eleusa* is the Icon of tenderness: the loving mother who arouses pity (eleos) in the beholder. The Mother of God is now affectionate towards the Son and towards the Faithful who look at him and recognize the Divinity in him.

---

205. Image: FRANTZ, R.A., public domain

Image 16, ref. 116

Panaghia Galaktotrophousa.[206]

In the Panaghia Galaktotrophousa, Maria offers her breast to the Child. She looks in front of her serious and sad, almost rigid, while all true tenderness comes from the Child. This type is also widespread in Russia and, in the West, the lactans Madonnas derive from it.

---

206. See: https://www.madredelbuonconsiglio.it/iconografia

Image 17, ref. 116

Panaghia Aghiosoritissa

The Panaghia Aghiosoritissa "is also known as the Intercession: it represents the Virgin almost in profile, with her arms outstretched in the act of intercession. Its prototype, attributed to Saint Luke, seems to have been brought to Constantinople from Palestine in the fifth century. It was probably lost in the course of the iconoclastic crisis. The Virgin may appear standing or in a three-quarter figure, but always alone, never with the Child. The type is in fact analogous to the Virgin of the Deesis, for this reason the figure is always turned towards its left, where ideally the Christ enthroned or on the cross should be found".[207]

---

[207]. See: http://www.liturgiabizantina.it/icone/testi/theotokos_2.htm

Image 18, ref. 118

From Panaghia Strastnaia the *Madonna del Perpetuo Soccorso (Our Lady of Perpetual Help)*, here protecting the hamlet of Fumone.

Image 19, ref. 118

St. Celestine V, on the left hand the village of Fumone, the right one blessing. On the side, the noble coat of arms of the Longhi-De Paolis family, owner of the Castle, in whose cell, dedicated to the Saint, the icon will be preserved.

Images 18 and 19: icons commissioned to the artist Sofia Nicoletti in October 2019 for the recurrence of the celebrations of Our Lady of Perpetual Help, which were held on 6 September 2020. The Committee intended to draw the attention of the faithful to the symbols of faith expressed in the icon that, since 1886, has been carried in a solemn procession through the alleys of the village. In the Oratory, destined until seventy years ago to celebrate funerals for those whose economic conditions did not allow the funeral in the Collegiate Church of SS. Annunziata (1147), located opposite, there is a room full of ex-votos. Dating back to the nineteenth century, they testify the great popular devotion to the icon which, through its intercession, is believed to have worked numerous miracles during the two world wars and in the immediate postwar period. Until about twenty years ago, the Icon was still very venerated. Over the years, many Fumonese emigrated far away, especially to North America, and today the veneration seems to be a bit dormant. Sacred vestments, the "stretcher of the company of a happy death", lights and processional crosses: it will be the responsibility of the Committee to restore everything and create a "Small museum of popular religiosity".

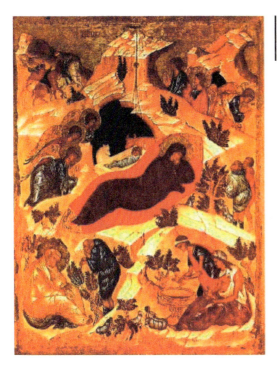

Image 20, ref. 124

Nativity Icon

In addition to the nativity of Christ, the icon represents the salient moments that accompanied the event: the three wise men, the angels, the shepherds, Joseph tempted by the evil one... However, we also see the women washing the child (the midwife Salome and the other – symbolically – Eva). All characters are apparently depicted without a precise order, on the sides of the icon. In fact, what is most significant is the black cave in the centre: a symbol of evil, darkness, in which the light of the newborn must shine. Something that, in order to happen, requires the resurrection of Christ: this is why the bands wrapping the newborn are, in fact, mortuary bandages. Christmas teaches that Christ came into the world to die on the cross and overcome death. It is not simply the birth of a child that must instill serenity, hope, the need for peace, as in the Catholic version. The crib becomes a sort of altar to which Jews and Gentiles, represented respectively by the donkey and the ox, are invited to eat. The bath scene is meant to indicate that Jesus is truly the son of man and recalls the rite of baptism (the tub has the shape of a baptismal font). In the thoughtful figure of Joseph is represented the human drama of temptation: before him the devil, in the guise of a shepherd (Tirso, from the Bacchantes' stick, in contrast with the trunk of Jesse, depicted next to the shepherd), is repeating to him: "in the same way that this stick cannot produce branches, so an old man like you cannot generate and, on the other hand, a virgin cannot give birth".

The angels face upwards, where a Trinitarian ray of light descends, while the last one on the right leans over the shepherds, to warn them of the event. In the centre the Virgin dominates majestically, lying on a purple cloth, who does not look at the newborn but at the destiny that awaits him and her as a mother (in some icons she looks at Joseph inviting him to resist temptation). All the figures surround it like a choir or a crown.[208]

Looking at the images through the centuries we notice this progressive rising of the Madonna, in the fourteenth century still lying down, then sitting and finally in the fifteenth century kneeling in adoration before the Child. According to Panovsky, "from the compositional point of view this change means the substitution of a triangular scheme for a rectangular one; from an iconographic point of view, it indicates the introduction of a new theme that will literally find its formulation in authors such as Pseudo-Bonaventura and Santa Brigida. But at the same time the innovation reveals a new emotional attitude, typical of the late stages of the Middle Ages".[209]

---

208. See: http://www.homolaicus.com/storia/medioevo/iconografia/93.htm

209. PANOFSKY, E. *Iconologia e Iconografia*, in *Il Significato nelle arti visive*, Einaudi, Torino, 1999, p. 35

Image 21, ref. 133

Christ crucified between Mary and St. John the Evangelist; wooden group; 1170-80; Bologna; Cathedral of St. Peter's.[210]

---

210. FRUGONI, C. *La voce delle immagini*, p. 4

Image 22, ref. 134

Gisleberto; The fate of the damned in hell.

Detail from the Last Judgment; stone bas-relief; XII century; Autun; Saint-Lazard Cathedral.[211]

---

211. Ibid., p. 6

Image 23, ref. 137

Beato de San Miguel de Escalada, Revelation chapters 12 and 13. Bifolium, c. 945, New York, Pierpont Morgan Library, M 644.

The Woman of the Apocalypse, at the top, on the left of the first bifolium, is rich in meanings: from the twelve stars that crown her head like twelve were the tribes of Israel, to the overturned moon under her feet to better reap the fruits of heaven. The popular tradition of lower Lazio has it that, hung on the walls of the house, she is able to keep the devil away.

"57. Chapter 12. And a great sign appeared in the sky: a woman surrounded by the sun, and the moon under her feet, and on her head a crown of twelve stars (chap. 12,1). It looks like this. The Madonna in the clouds with a flaming dress and angel's wings, and around her crown twelve stars, and all around her rays of sunshine from head to foot, and under her feet the moon, and in front of her a red dragon with seven heads and seven diadems and ten horns that he sends out of his mouth water like a river, and the earth, opening up swallows the river, and behind the tail of the monster a quantity of stars, and above the Madonna two angels who carry Christ the Child in a cloth, and around them many clouds".[212]

---

212. DA FURNÀ, D. *Canone dell'icona. Il manuale di arte sacra dei monaci del Monte Athos*, Pentàgora, Savona 2014, p. 187

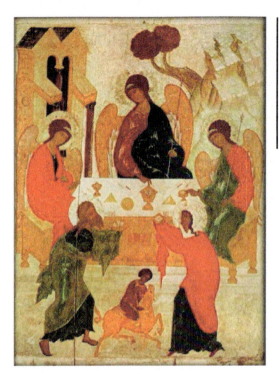

Image 24, ref. 140

Hospitality of Abraham. Novgorod school XV century. Abraham and Sarah serve the three pilgrims while the servant kills the calf to sacrifice in honor of the three who came.[213]

---

213. See: https://slideplayer.it/slide/926865/

Image 25, ref. 140
Andrej Rublëv; 1422.[214]

---

214. See: https://it.aleteia.org/2017/06/09/icona-russa-mistero-trinita/

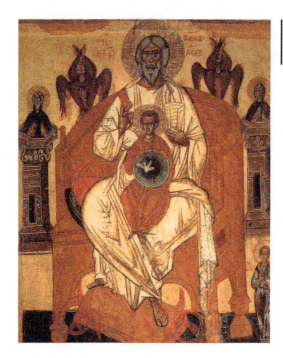

Image 26, ref. 140

Icon of Fatherhood.[215]

---

215. See: http://www.sentiericona.it/public/icone/?p=936

Image 27, ref. 149

Beato Angelico, Annunciation, 1433-34; Prado Museum, Madrid.[216]

The representation is divided into three parts to signal the presence of the Holy Trinity. In this version, the relationship between the new Eve, Mary and the old Eve is highlighted, at the bottom of the Garden of Eden, on the left, looking towards her "advocata". At the intersection of the pendentives of the capitals, God the Father also looks in the direction of the Virgin, as does the Spirit who illuminates her with a ray of light. Everyone is waiting for that "Ecce", in response to the "Where are you" expected, in the Economy of Salvation, for centuries by all of humanity.

"He was called Beato Angelico for his ability to recreate the angelic atmosphere that surrounded the religious subjects he portrayed in his paintings, renewing sacred art in the fifteenth century according to the nascent Renaissance vision to which he adhered in a sublime way in terms of light, color and spiritual grace. In the last moments of life, he aimed long and high, almost transfiguring his face with emotion; then he exclaimed: "The Madonna is much more beautiful than I painted her!" And he expired. It is significant that Fra Giovanni is the only artist, in the entire history of the Church, in whose canonical process no theological or spiritual writings were attached but the complete catalog of his masterpieces of art and faith. John Paul II on February 18, 1984 proclaimed him Universal Patron of Artists".[217]

---

216. See: http://mauriziobianchi.blogspot.com/2013/04/annunciazione-pittori-del-1400.html

217. See: http://www.adelaidetrabucco.it/ index.php? option = com_k2&view = item&id = 73:iconografia-rosariana

Beato Angelico manages to represent the *kénosis* of the Virgin or the emptying of oneself to make room for the divine Logos in the incarnation: an indispensable and functional premise for the encounter with Christ by grace and the Spirit. The Virgin presents herself to God as poor, free from all worldly burdens, aiming exclusively at a spiritual fruitfulness, fruit of divine love, but at the moment of the Annunciation Mary discovers that her poverty has been transformed by the Lord into wealth: she will be the Virgin Mother of the Son of the Highest. Later, she will also discover that her motherhood is destined to extend to all men whom the Son has come to save: she will give birth to all of humanity. Christ Incarnate is the perfect work of art, directly painted by God in union with a woman, Mary.

Image 28, ref. 168

A battle of the Reconquista.[218]

---

218. See: http://www.cantigasdesantamaria.com

Bibliography

Augustine, *Il maestro e la parola*, Bompiani, Milan, 2010
Arendt, H. *Il concetto di storia: nell'antichità e oggi*, in Arendt, H. *Tra passato e futuro*, Garzanti, Milan, 1991
Baudry, G.H. *Simboli cristiani delle origini. I-VII secolo*, Jaca Book, Milan, 2016
Bonaventura, *La sapienza cristiana. Collationes in Hexaëmeron*, Collatio XV, Jaca Book, Milan, 1985
Cardini, F. *Europa e Islam, storia di un malinteso*, Laterza, Bari, 2010
Cassirer, E. *Saggio sull'uomo. Introduzione ad una filosofia della cultura umana*, Armando, Rome, 2009
Clement, O. *Memorie di speranza. Intervista di Jean-Claude Noyer*, tr. it., Jaca Book, Milan, 2006
Coppa, G. *Sant'Ambrogio*, Opere Utet, Turin, 1979
Cusano, N. *La dotta ignoranza*, Città Nuova, Rome, 2011
Da Furnà, D. *Canone dell'icona. Il manuale di arte sacra dei monaci del Monte Athos*, Pentàgora, Savona 2014
Damascene, J. *Adversus eos qui sacras imagines abiciunt*, in *Opera Omnia*, ed. Migne, Paris, 1862
Danto, A.C. *Che cos'è l'arte*, Johan & Levi, 2017
De Chardin, P. T. *Sulla felicità*, Queriniana, 2013
De Simone G. *La devozione popolare tra arte e teologia*, Nuova serie Quaderni dell'arte e teologia, 2019
Di Sardi, M. *Sulla Pasqua*, ca. AD 190
Dulaey, M. *I simboli cristiani. Catechesi e Bibbia (I-IV secolo)*, Edizioni San Paolo, 2004
Eco, U. *Storia della bruttezza*, Bompiani, Milan, 2013
Evdokìmov, P.N. *L'Ortodossia*, EDB, 2016
Florenskij, P.A. *Le porte regali*, Marsilio, Venice, 2018
Frugoni, C. *La voce delle immagini. Pillole iconografiche dal Medioevo*, Einaudi, Turin, 2010
Guastini Carrocci, D. *Poetica*, Rome, 2010
Guénon, R. *Simboli della scienza sacra*, Adelphi, 1990
Hamilton, G. *The art & Archtecture of Russia*, Yale University Press, 1992
Heidegger, M. *Che cos'è metafisica?* (1929, edited by Franco Volpi), Adelphi, 2006
Heidegger, M. *Lettera sull'«umanismo»*, Adelphi, Milan, 1995
Heidegger, M. *Unterwegs zur Sprache*, Pfullingen, Neske, 1959
Hölderlin, F. *Iperione*, Feltrinelli, 2013
Holland, T. *Millennium. Re, predoni, cavalieri e la nascita della cristianità*, il Saggiatore, Milan, 2013
Kant, I. *Critica alla facoltà di giudizio*, Einaudi, Turin, 2011
Maimonide, M. *La Guida Dei Perplessi*, LXI, edited by M. Zonta, Turin, Utet, 2003
Marion, J.L. *Dio senza essere*, Jaca Book, Milan, 2018

Maritain, J. *Christianity and Democracy*, Charles Scribner's Sons, New York, 1950
Maritain, J. *L'intuizione creativa nell'arte e nella poesia*, Morcelliana, Brescia, 2016
Matvejević, P. *Breviario mediterraneo*, Garzanti, Milan, 2006
Mirri, L. *Icona la bellezza rivelata. Suggestioni teologiche dell'icona*, Biblioteca Francescana, Milan 2015
Moro, J. *Il sari rosso, Il Saggiatore*, Milan 2010
Onasch, K. *Die Ikonenmalerei*, Koehler-Amelang, Leipzig 1968
Panovsky E. *Iconologia e Iconografia*, in *Il Significato nelle arti visive*, Turin, 1999
Pareyson, L. *Filosofia della libertà*, Il melagolo, Genoa, 1991
Pastoureau, M. *Bestiari del Medioevo*, Einaudi, Turin, 2010
Piccolo, G. *Fatti di parole. Filosofia del linguaggio*, GBP, Rome, 2019
Piccolo, G. *Il gioco dei frammenti. Raccontare l'enigma dell'identità*, San Paolo, 2020
Piccolo, G.; Sebastiani, M. *La devozione popolare tra Arte e Teologia. Idolo e Icona* (ed. Giuseppina De Simone), Nuova serie Quaderni di arte e teologia, 2019
Plato, *Cratylus*
Plato, *Phaedrus*, ca. 370 BC
Plato, *Symposium*, ca. 385–370 BC
Plato, *The Republic*, ca. 375 BC
Ricoeur, P. *Il simbolo dà a pensare*, Morcelliana, Brescia, 2002
Sendler, E. *L'icona immagine dell'invisibile. Elementi di teologia, estetica e tecnica*, San Paolo, Milan, 1985
Špidlik, T. *Alcune considerazioni sulla teologia dell'icona*, in *Al principio era l'arte*, Lipa, Rome, 2006
Špidlik, T.; Rupnik M.I. *Parola e immagine*, Lipa, Rome, 1995
Stein, E. *Il problema dell'empatia*, Studium, Rome, 2018
Thomas Aquinas, *Summa Theologiae*, ca. 1265–1274
Walter, I.F.; Wolf, N. *Capolavori della miniatura. I codici miniati più belli del mondo dal 400 al 1600*, Taschen, Köln, 2003
Wittgenstein, L. *Ricerche filosofiche*, Prima parte, Einaudi, Turin, 1995
Von Balthasar, H. U. *Gloria. La percezione della forma; un'estetica teologica*, vol I, Jaca Book, Milan, 2012
Exhibition catalogue: *Andy Warhol*, Brasini Wing, Vittoriano complex, Rome, 2019

Biblical Sources
Apocalypse
Exodus
Genesis
John
Isaiah
Luke
Tobias

Sacred Books
Sura, XIV-XV

Letters and Homilies
Fathers of the Second Vatican Council to artists, 8 December 1965
Pope BENEDICT XVI, Speech of 21 November 2009
Pope FRANCIS in his homily at Casa Santa Marta on Friday 14 February 2020; on family and love
Pope PAUL VI, Apostolic Exhortation Evangelii nuntiandi
Pope JOHN PAUL II, Letter to the artists, 4 April 1999

Webography
(In alphabetical order – Last consultation: 31.03.2021)

academia.edu

adelaidetrabucco.it

cantigasdesantamaria.com

gianfrancobertagni.it

homolaicus.com

iconemirabile.wordpress.com

immaculate.one

it.aleteia.org

laciviltacattolica.it

latheotokos.it

liturgiabizantina.it

madredelbuonconsiglio.it

mauriziobianchi.blogspot.com

notedipastoralegiovanile.it

santiebeati.it

sentiericona.it

slideplayer.it

sufi.it

treccani.it

turismo.it

vaticannews.va

youtube.com

List of Images

1. William Holman Hunt; *The Light of the World*, 1853-1854. Keble College, Oxford
2. Andy Warhol, Campbell's Soup, screen printing
3. Philip Augustus expels the Jews from France, miniature, after 1321, Brussels, Bibliothèque Royale, ms 6931 (5), f. 265r.
4. Map of Bedolina; Upper Paleolithic
5. Minangkabau, Sumatra Island, Indonesia. Cosmogony as a representation of meaning
6. Allegory of the hill of Wisdom. Siena Cathedral. Pinturicchio, dating from around 1505.
7. Caravaggio, Rest on the Flight into Egypt, 1596, detail. Doria Pamphilj Gallery, Rome
8. Matera; Crypt of the Original Sin
9. Codex Aureus Epternacensis. Gospel of Echternach; 1030 approx.; Benedictine Abbey of Echternach; Client Abbot Humbert of Echterbach; Nuremberg, Germanisches Nationalmuseum, Hs. 156142.
10. The colours of the Panther; 1240 circa, Michel Pastoureau, Bestiaries of the Middle Ages, 10
11. Panaghia Platytera
12. Processional icon of Maria Odigitria among prophets, 1512-13, from Vallacchia
13. Panaghia Nikopoia
14. Panaghia Glykophilousa
15. Eleusa
16. Panaghia Galaktotrophousa
17. Panaghia Aghiosoritissa
18. Panaghia Strastnaia, Madonna del Perpetuo Soccorso
19. Celestine V
20. Nativity Icon
21. Christ crucified between Mary and St. John the Evangelist; wooden group; 1170-80; Bologna; Cathedral of St. Peter's.

22. Gisleberto; The fate of the damned in hell. Detail from the Last Judgment; stone bas-relief; XII century; Autun; Saint-Lazard Cathedral.

23. Beato de San Miguel de Escalada, Revelation chapters 12 and 13. Bifoglio c.945, New York, Pierpont Morgan Library, M 644.

24. Hospitality of Abraham Novgorod school XV century.

25. Andrej Rublëv; 1422

26. Icon of Fatherhood

27. Beato Angelico, Annunciation, 1433-34; Prado Museum, Madrid

28. A battle of the *Reconquista*

Index

Preface (by Ulrich van Loyen), p. 9

Introduction (by the author), p. 13

Chapter 1, Mousiké and Myth, p. 25
    1.1 Poetic Intuition in the Work of Art, p. 27
    1.2 The Work of Art in Dialogue with the Myth, p. 31

Chapter 2, Thinking Above is Thinking the Limit, p. 33
    2.1 The Kantian *Sensus Communis*, p. 35
    2.2 The Story of Peoples, p. 37

Chapter 3, Being and Nothing, p. 39
    3.1 Let Nothing Be, p. 41
    3.2 God Chose to "Write the Icon", p. 44

Chapter 4, Memory, Hope, p. 49
    4.1 The Icon Reflects the Shape of Humanity, p. 51

Chapter 5, *Symbolon* Versus *Diaballo*, p. 53
    5.1 The Meaning of the Symbol from its Origins, p. 55
    5.2 The Divine Name, p. 56
    5.3 In Metaphorical Symbolism We Recognise "He Who Is", p. 60

Chapter 6, Aim and Appear, p. 65
    6.1 Idol and Icon, p. 67
    6.2 The Idol According to Marion, p. 68
    6.3 The Icon, p. 70

Chapter 7, The Dogma of Incarnation in the Icon, p. 73
    7.1 The Germs of Iconoclasm, p. 75
    7.2 Christian Art: Dogmas Translated into Art, p. 77
    7.3 Outbreak of the Crisis and Resolution, p. 81

Chapter 8, The Theories of the Image, p. 85
    8.1 The Theories of the Image. East and West, p. 87
    8.2 Image as Participation in the Divine, p. 88
    8.3 Image as a Sign, p. 91

Chapter 9, The Byzantine Icon, p. 93
    9.1 The Canon of the Icon, p. 95
    9.2 Literary Genres of Icons, p. 97
    9.2.1 *The Panegyric Model*, p. 97
    9.2.2 *The Epic Model*, p. 101
    9.2.3 *The Dramatic Model*, p. 102
    9.2.4 *The Model of the Theological Treatise*, p. 106

Chapter 10, Light and Perspective, p. 109
    10.1 The Icon Rejects the Real, p. 111
    10.2 The Beautiful and the Sublime, p. 112
    10.3 Natural Light and Spiritual Light, p. 115

Conclusions, p. 117

The Word to Images, p. 131

Bibliography, p. 165
    Biblical Sources, p. 167
    Sacred Books, p. 167
    Letters and Homilies, p. 167
    Webography, p. 168

List of Images, p. 169

Acknowledgments, p. 177

Acknowledgments

Giving thanks means "giving back", expressing gratitude for the good received.

I therefore give the first thanks to the Mother of God: she is majestic, powerful, she never runs out of Her strength, even when mine would like to yield. She stands beside me and supports me. You will say, "this statement is anachronistic!". I understand. A few years ago, I would have thought the same. I come from a normal family of our days, we have always proclaimed ourselves Catholics without ever questioning the intimate and profound meaning of our Creed.

I could not indicate a certain beginning to this question of mine. It could coincide with the prayer to the Guardian Angel that my grandmother made me recite at the end of each day. I felt safe. I could then close my eyes and abandon myself to the darkness of the night: the Angel would have taken care of me and my brothers, and the pitfalls vanished. Otherwise, I could think of a closer time when, as president of Cultural Association *La Melusina*, with the intention of revealing the Middle Ages to children through targeted workshops, I met Sacred art, in particular the Icon, and through the study of gestures and symbols in relation to the Word I discovered the Book: once opened, to understand, the rest came by itself.

Seeing is believing! The latter period found a strong acceleration with the ascent to the papal throne of Pope Francis. I then discovered a Church that I thought did not exist, a Church that welcomes me too, with all my shortcomings. And my wandering through works of art soon turned into a pilgrimage, following millenary paths traced by those who, before me, set out on their way to the Gate of Heaven; the traces are clearly visible on this land, the deep furrows, if you get lost you can resume the road. I therefore turn with grateful heart to that man dressed in white, who has come here from the other side of the world, with a foreign name pronounced differently by each one but each one feels called by him, because Jorge Mario Bergoglio talks about universal Love, the same one that Jesus preached.

A feeling of special gratitude goes to my family, together with me on the way; to my children, Filippo and Sofia, and to my husband Maurizio, who supports me with love in my passionate study.

Continuing on, I cannot fail to return with a grateful heart to the *Università Pontificia Gregoriana*. A world in the world, under that quadrangle everyone is encouraged to bring out the best for themselves, helped by colleagues and accompanied by professors whose goal is wisdom, knowledge is not enough. I feel especially grateful to Father Gaetano Piccolo, now Dean of the Faculty of Philosophy. He never categorised my many questions as pedantic or out of place, even if, I understand now, they sometimes seemed absurd to him. On the contrary, he urged me, placed more and more in the question, to accept the position of supervisor of my thesis: my first timid attempt to respond to gestures and symbols that risk oblivion.

What I mean, and this is what I hope to have conveyed in the pages of this book on the origins and meaning of the Sacred Icons, is that sometimes we believe out of habit, perhaps because our grandparents taught us, and we follow rites that are no longer included in our universe of meaning, with meaning buried in the dust of time. We repeat without understanding millennial gestures, or at most we believe they are rites to be protected, "curious material" for an anthropological study. The invitation is to "remain in the question", those millenary rites, the meaning behind each symbol, are precious, precisely because they belong to the origins of Christianity, whose story coincides with our identity as a people, to be rediscovered in order to rediscover ourselves, and knowingly decide whether to "keep the Promise". Repeating them automatically certainly serves not to forget, understanding them means living the Faith in the incessant search for meaning.

The West that was Christian is experiencing a worrying identity crisis: we have demolished ideologies, there are no longer any parties within which to act for the common good, we feel a strong desire for spirituality, but we no longer find it in our tradition. We therefore wander like "masks in search of an author", fearing all diversity because we no longer know how to recognize ourselves: we have lost the foundation legend that "In the beginning" our fathers assumed to become a "We". It is only as members of a community that men prepare themselves for action, and communities are different from each other, obey different laws, have different habits and customs, venerate different memories of their past, we witness a fruitful multiplicity of traditions. What all these various forms of human plurality have in common is the simple fact of their origin: at a precise point in time and for some reason a group of people have come to represent themselves as a "We".

That enormous variety of human societies can be thought of as united in the mystery of that "In the beginning", which makes us all children of one God: different from each other but brothers, united in charity, therefore in "taking care" of each other and the common home. "Taking care of the world around us and supporting us means taking care of ourselves. But we need to constitute ourselves in a we who inhabits the common home", as Pope Francis recalls in the *Encyclical Fratelli Tutti (All Brothers)*.

Father Piccolo, as well as Professor Andrea Di Maio, Professor Ramón Lucas Lucas and many others at Gregoriana, understood my wandering and helped me to systematise it in a path of study and research; I was one of these masks in search of an author: today my face is fully in the Project for the "construction of the Common Home".

Thank you!

The Author

Lucia De Carolis is a philosopher, writer and freelance journalist. She holds a degree from the *Pontificia Università Gregoriana*, in Rome, and is currently candidate to a Master's degree in Philosophy and Aesthetics from the same university.

In 2020 she has curated the exhibition "Icon and Popular Piety", held in the fortress of Fumone, with images and texts on the history of popular piety and icons by artist Sofia Nicoletti.

Contact:

luciadecarolis@gmail.com

Printed in Great Britain
by Amazon